User E
An intro
interac

Published in Great Britain by

Laurence King Student & Professional
An imprint of Quercus Editions Ltd
Carmelite House
50 Victoria Embankment
London EC4Y 0DZ

An Hachette UK company

A CIP catalogue record for this book is available from the
British Library

TPB ISBN 978-1-52942-026-5
EBOOK ISBN 978-1-52942-027-2

10 9 8 7 6 5 4 3 2 1

Design: Blok Graphic
Project editor: Jodi Simpson
Commissioning editor: Liz Faber

Printed and bound in China by C&C Offset Printing Co., Ltd.

Mark Wells

User Experience Design

An introduction
to creating
interactive
digital spaces

Laurence King Publishing

'Design is not just what it looks like and feels like. Design is how it works.'

Steve Jobs

Contents

Introduction to digital user experience design

This book is for you if you are studying a creative visual subject that encompasses user experience (UX) design or if you have a creative background and want to gain a broad understanding of UX design as it relates to digital and hybrid environments with a user focus. It will examine some of the most used design approaches and how to harness these to create engaging solutions for a client, explore different ways of identifying and understanding the audience for your product, and help you develop the content and visual interface for your product. It will help you build upon your pre-existing skills to create innovative, engaging and exciting products that utilize screen-based digital solutions.

Don Norman, one of the first people to use the term *user experience*, defines UX as being 'everything . . . and how you experience it'; it concerns the whole of a user's journey, not just a single experience of using, for example, a website. Jakob Nielsen, a foremost expert in the field, reinforces this definition by saying that 'UX is people' – it is not about technology or computers, but about users and the design team who create the solutions. Nielsen identifies three constant principles in UX, which inform the key areas of this book: understand the user, test ideas and use iterative design.

Throughout the book a range of terminology is used to reference what you are creating for people to interact with: most often, this is called a *product*. Traditionally, when we think of products or product design we think of tangible three-dimensional objects, but the term *product* has developed and now also encompasses virtual objects: for example, traditional websites, augmented or virtual reality, or even voice user interfaces, in one form or another – these are all products that you, as a UX designer, might create.

The sections of the book reflect the basic UX design process:
1. Understanding
2. Research, discovery, analysis and definition
3. Development.

Part 1: 'Methods and approaches' unpacks and clarifies different methods for and approaches to solving design problems; helps you understand your client and what they want from you, create design briefs and develop a good working relationship with your client and other members of your team; and explores the possibilities of different platforms you can use to engage with your audience.

Part 2: 'Knowing your audience' explains how to identify and get to know your audience through user research, including data collection and analysis; learn how to present your findings in the most effective

Digital design does not always take place on a screen.

ways, using visuals and storytelling; use your research to deepen your understanding of your users by creating personas, user stories, journey maps and empathy maps; and undertake user testing to help you pinpoint any problems and inform further iterations of your concepts.

Part 3: 'Refining your product' examines considerations in designing digital interfaces across multiple devices, perhaps even going beyond the screen by incorporating voice commands or augmented or virtual reality; plan your content effectively, ensuring that it works just as well as your visual design and supports search engine optimization and other strategies for differentiating you from your competition and driving traffic to your product; and create prototypes to visualize your product and help you refine and troubleshoot your design.

UX design skills are highly transferable, and UX design approaches can be applied across a broad range of disciplines. The book contains extensive examples of work ranging from art-based to commercial projects, both large and small scale, to show you what you can achieve and to give you a good understanding of what is possible in commercial environments. Case studies of projects by practising designers give further insight. The book introduces you to the fundamentals required of a UX designer, as well as skills you need and other aspects of the design process that you should be aware of in order to work successfully with a team and manage client relationships.

'UX is people. It's not technology, it's not about computers, it's about people.'

Jakob Nielsen, usability pioneer

methods & approaches

12–55

1.1 Design methods

There are hundreds of different approaches that can be taken to solving digital design problems. When you've just received a brief or started a new project, knowing where to start and which methods are appropriate and most effective for a particular product can save you a lot of time and trouble. In this section, we look at a few key design methods and use these as a starting point to explore how we go about crafting solutions specifically for a digital audience.

While the idea of a design process implies that there is a set list of steps to follow to produce solutions, you should never consider anything to be set in stone. Ultimately, the design process is creative and about solving problems; it is a guide to making sense of something that, at first, appears to be an incomprehensible mass of questions; it is a way of thinking (fig. 1).

1 The design process is not linear – it is full of twists and turns.

Every design project is going to have ups and downs, and you will most certainly feel all at sea at times, but the skill lies in recognizing

this and understanding the best way to navigate your way through. One way is to signpost key parts of the journey and map it out before you begin so that you have a rough path to follow. The design process can be seen as a collection of milestones and tools that you can use to help you resolve a design brief. Each design brief will require a slightly different approach, with emphasis placed on different processes, principles or tools.

While there can be no specific formula for a design method that answers every brief – that would be no fun and create some very strange solutions! – there are a number of design methods that can help you form a framework that you can use to navigate a broad range of projects. These include the Design Council's framework for innovation, IDEO's human-centred design approach and GV's design sprint. Each of these uses a mixture of both critical and creative thinking to help create successful outcomes.

The waterfall approach

The traditional model of product development, known as the water-fall approach (fig. 2), is one that you may recognize, even if you've seen it with slightly different wording:

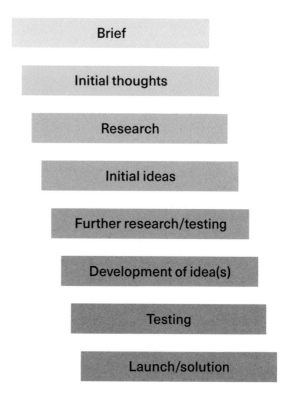

Brief

Initial thoughts

Research

Initial ideas

Further research/testing

Development of idea(s)

Testing

Launch/solution

2 The traditional waterfall approach.

This approach implies that design is a linear process, but nothing could be further from the truth. Finding a solution to a brief is messy, and even if you use the same design method every time, the nuances of the method, and therefore the outcome, will be different. Being messy and non-linear means that you may experience both moments of frustration and times of elation. But it also gives you an opportunity to bring in different approaches to finding solutions.

Collaborative approaches

As the design field has developed and changed, so have the approaches to it. Design now has a greater emphasis on collaboration with both experts and the audience you are creating solutions for. Co-creation, co-design or participatory design, design thinking and human-centred design are approaches that have collaboration as their foundation. These methods are often written about because they transfer well to areas outside of the creative arena and therefore have become popular in business. Often businesses use design thinking as a framework to understand issues and find solutions.

Co-creation is an approach in which the users frequently play a key role in shaping a solution or product with the company who is making it. In *co-design*, or what is traditionally called *participatory design*, the users play a role in the design aspect of a project. *Design thinking* uses creativity as a means to solve problems and is much more user-solution focused. All these approaches are focused on working with and not for each other.

Design thinking is broader than just visual design and can be used for a whole range of tasks. Part of design thinking is putting people/users at the heart of finding solutions. IDEO is a global design company that has embraced design thinking and specifically *human-centred design* (HCD) as an approach to finding solutions. IDEO defines design thinking as 'a way to solve problems through creativity'.

The following methods and approaches, in one way or another, encapsulate elements of design thinking, co-creation, and co-design or participatory design.

Design sprints

At Google, and then at GV (previously known as Google Ventures), Jake Knapp developed the design sprint (fig. 3). This process was used to create products including Gmail and Hangouts.

GV uses design sprints to focus on design, prototyping and testing – not building or launching. Design sprints are not only for digital-based products; they can be used to develop other kinds of products, education, architecture and much more. GV describes the process as 'a "greatest hits" of business strategy, innovation, behaviour science, design thinking, and more'.

Design sprints bring together a group to work on exploring and finding a solution to a problem. The group does not need to be a

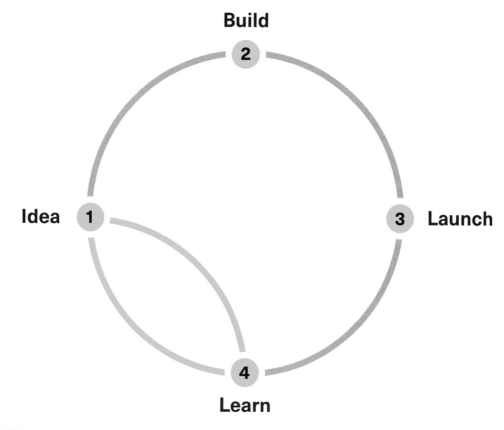

3 GV's design sprint process.

pre-existing team, and it is often beneficial to include a variety of voices to help explore and generate ideas. A design sprint can give a broad range of people the opportunity to contribute – unlike traditional brainstorming sessions, which can sometimes result in only the loudest person getting their ideas across. It also gives the opportunity to build client relationships and understand a client's product and customers in more depth. But design sprints are not intended to follow an idea to completion, so they often sit within a much larger process of researching, developing and launching products.

Once an idea or initial concept has been formed, a design sprint is often used to identify issues and generate solutions. Because of the relatively large investment of people and time, a design sprint is often worthwhile for a big challenge that needs dedicated time to investigate and resolve. The challenge does not necessarily need to involve new ideas, it can be about refining and developing pre-existing ideas. A design sprint is often run across one or two weeks (although this can vary) and aims to have a set of proposals or prototypes as an outcome.

During a design sprint, a group will come together to work through a series of key stages:

- **Identify problems and pinpoint initial directions by mapping out what they want to achieve**
- **Identify how they might achieve their goals and what challenges they may face along the way**
- **Through reflective questioning, identify key stakeholders who, through informal interviews, may be able to help answer and resolve some of the questions**
- **Sketch out and discuss potential solutions**
- **Review the potential ideas and critique them in preparation for prototyping and testing on an audience.**

'True collaboration isn't throwing designs over the wall. It's designers, engineers, and the rest of the team sharing the responsibility to build a quality product.'

Diana Mounter, head of design at GitHub

Engagement

Connecting the dots and building relationships
between different citizens, stakeholders and partners.

DESIGN PRINCIPLES

1. Be People Centred
2. Communicate (visually & Inclusively)
3. Collaborate & Co-Create
4. Iterate, Iterate, Iterate

Challenge

Outcome

Discover

Define

Develop

Deliver

METHODS BANK

Explore, Shape, Build

Creating the connections that allow innovation,
including culture change, skills and mindset.

Leadership

4 The Design Council's framework for innovation.

The framework for innovation

Known as the framework for innovation (fig. 4), the Design Council's methodology aims to 'achieve significant and long-lasting positive change'. It is used by a range of organizations and, similar to design thinking and design sprints, is user focused and has reflection and iteration at the core of its approach – it involves making, testing and putting the user first. However, unlike the design sprint, it covers the whole design process rather than just concentrating on the testing and ideas stage. The framework has been used by companies in areas from transport to education. It is ideal for projects including a range of different groups, who can be brought in at key stages to help inform the direction of the project.

The original 'double diamond' diagram that the Design Council created to describe their framework was beautifully simple, though in many ways it was too simple and implied that the approach had a relative formulaic approach. But it also enabled key members of projects outside of design teams to begin to understand the process that designers go through in order to produce outcomes. This enabled the framework for innovation to be understood and used by other groups to 'tackle some of the most complex social, economic and environmental problems'. The framework is particularly effective in projects that have many key stakeholders exploring challenges in different disciplines who can come together to create a collaborative solution that is user focused.

1.2 Digital design methods

In the previous section we looked at design methods that are not exclusive to digital products. This section will look at some approaches that, while still transferable, are unique to the digital space.

Design for a digital space brings a unique set of challenges. A good place to start is with Gillian Crampton Smith's basics of good interaction design, which you can use as the beginning of a framework for digital user experience design. In fact, you can use the following list to quickly and easily interrogate many interactive objects, from fire alarms to websites.

Good interaction design gives us

- **A clear mental model** of what we're interacting with.
- **Reassuring feedback**, so that we know what we've done and when we have done it.
- **Navigability**, especially with things that are on screen. You need to know where you are in the system, what you can do there, where you can go next and how to get back.
- **Consistency**, so that the same response is experienced in different places of the system.
- **Intuitive interaction**, which minimizes the burden of conscious thought needed to operate the system, leaving us to concentrate on our goals.

- **Responsive behaviour and quality**, to design not just what it looks like, but how it behaves, and the quality of how we interact with it in the right context.

The waterfall approach in the digital space

In the traditional waterfall approach to product design (see 'The waterfall approach', p. 13), each stage of a project does not overlap and is largely independent; once a stage is finished by a team and handed to the next team, the next stage can begin, and the two never really cross over. When it comes to working collaboratively and developing new digital solutions, this is a dysfunctional, slow and arduous process. A company using this approach to respond to an identified issue or change in the market may then take such a long time to make a change to its product that the updated product may already be out of date by the time it launches.

The waterfall approach does have its place in digital design (fig. 5), though it is 'only appropriate for some types of system'. For example, the waterfall approach can be useful in safety-critical systems, large software systems and embedded systems where digital and physical systems have to work together. Software developers, however, often look beyond the waterfall approach to different methods, such as the agile mindset and the incremental model, which we will look at next.

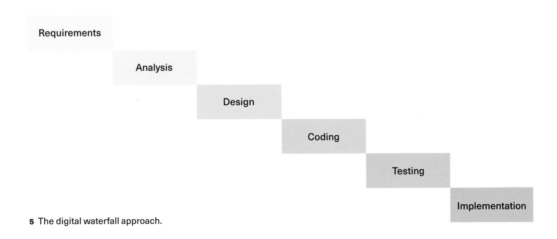

5 The digital waterfall approach.

The agile mindset

Agile design is iterative – that is, it has distinct cycles of development that are repeated – and fast paced (fig. 6). The basis of the concept is that it creates a quicker response time to developing solutions by constantly improving a product (e.g., a website) through smaller, rather than longer, cycles of development. This enables new features driven by user testing, changes in the market or developments in technology to be released much more quickly. For this reason, it tends to be the design method of choice for software developers.

In an agile development model, it is common to deliver working solutions to end users, often based on the idea of user stories or features. For example, rather than a website being updated one element at a time, user stories, which address the process a user goes through as they use a product, are implemented (for more on user stories, see 'Storytelling', p. 87). The iterative nature of the agile approach means that a digital product or solution might be released before it is final; this is why you'll often see 'alpha' and 'beta' or 'preview' on public-facing apps and websites. The challenge with agile approaches is keeping track of the end goal and the overall architecture and structure of the solution. A good agile development process transfers this burden on to good product managers and systems architects.

6 The agile development cycle.

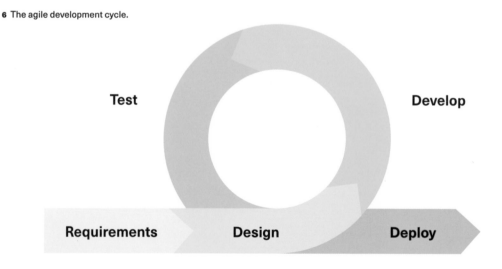

Test

Develop

Requirements

Design

Deploy

The agile mindset also uses sprints, not dissimilar to design sprints (see 'Design sprints', p. 15). Agile sprints are kept short (one to four weeks, normally two) to ensure that focus on the end user and on outcomes is maintained. Normally you would get user feedback after every sprint, or during the following sprint. Some sprints may be focused on prototyping and others on development, but there should be an element of design, development and testing in every agile sprint.

The processes of the agile mindset may look similar to those of other approaches, but they are carried out in much smaller, more focused cycles, rather than one single cycle for a whole overarching project. The agile approach is responsive and reactive to the environment it is in, rather than reflective and holistic.

The incremental model

This incremental model (fig. 7) is not dissimilar to the agile process, and there is significant overlap between the two, though the incremental model has longer cycles and a larger, more holistic view of the creation of a system. From one set of requirements a series of increments is generated, structured so that each builds on the previous one: for example, each increment may release new features

7 The incremental model.

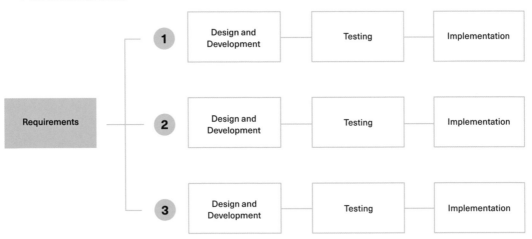

Iterative

Incremental

Iterative and incremental

to a product. However, each increment has its own cycle of design and development, testing and implementation.

The scrum process

While scrum is not in itself a design methodology, it is related to the agile mindset, the incremental model and design sprints (fig. 8). Scrum is not dissimilar to agile, but its focus is on the organization of a project and how a team works together rather than on the product or solution the team is creating (fig. 9). Scrum creates transparency between developers and wider organizations and helps to create non-hierarchical teams where projects are broken down into manageable tasks.

A scrum team is made up of no more than seven members, and work is undertaken in cycles of sprints of two to four weeks, with the product owner deciding what the priorities are and how the challenge should be specified, such as through a user story. A set of tasks for the project, known as a product backlog, is created, and the team as a whole selects the highest priority items to work on. The sprint will take place for a set period of time, and if an item is not completed it will be fed back into the product backlog. During the sprint updates, problems and issues are shared in quick daily team meetings.

8 Design processes can be iterative (like the agile mindset), incremental (like the incremental model), or both.

9 The scrum process.

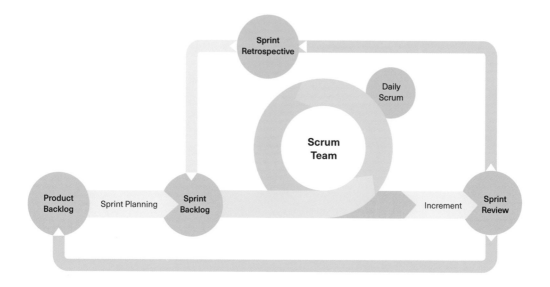

The scrum process is easily transferable to areas outside of development and has become a popular framework for design sprint teams.

Design systems

A design system is similar to brand guidelines that outline how a brand's visual assets should be used, but a little more complicated because it incorporates a number of other components and has a focus on user experience. Design systems evolved from the need to bring together different elements that are specifically required in a digital design and development environment. For this reason, design systems are considered a digital design method.

Design systems have a number of reusable components with clear standards that enable them to be used to create a consistent experience across different solutions (fig. 10). They are continually refined and updated. Essentially, a design system is a living, breathing toolkit, and all teams who need to engage with the design system must be aware of it and buy into it – there is no point working hard as a team to create a design system and then not getting it out into the company and believing in it. As part of a design system's creation and revisions, users should be consulted at appropriate points of the development cycle, as these are ultimately the people who are going to be experiencing it.

Alongside visual elements that form the identity of a company, a design system can include principles, best practices, documentation, user interfaces (sometimes referred to as a pattern library), code, editorial guidelines and more. Because of the range of components involved in a design system, it is something that often sits across the full range of disciplines – including developers, engineers, visual designers and content creators – within a team, meaning that everyone has a role to play in using the design system and no one discipline owns it. This ensures a common goal across the company and brings a synergy to all areas while ultimately being good for the user experience.

The design system also has the benefit of being flexible, so that it can be implemented in ways that are appropriate for a specific brief while keeping the elements of the brand consistent. It also enables rapid prototyping and iterations, because the components – graphical, code and other kinds – are already created. This is particularly important with expectation and demand within companies increasing the speed at which products are developed and launched.

It is often difficult to envision all the possible ways that a brand's assets may be used. However, having common elements that can be used across different platforms and in new spaces leads to consistency across different products and platforms – even ones that have not yet been created. This is a natural evolution from products such as brand guidelines and has come about primarily because of the development and demands of the digital environment. The design system enables a holistic overview so that the many facets of a company do not become segmented and in doing so creates consistency – especially when there are multiple teams and products involved, and when products have to behave in similar ways.

10 Components of Google's Material Design system.

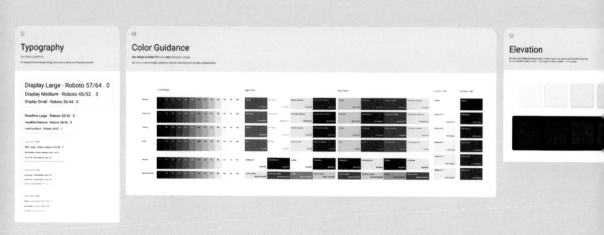

Design systems

Tessa Rodes was the senior design manager of the IBM Cloud PAL system. In 2013 she was part of the first group to go through the IBM Design programme, which transformed IBM's company culture by embedding designers in all key product teams.

Nick Hahn is the director of design systems consulting at InVision. Previously he worked at IBM, and before that in advertising. He has worked in UX design since it was developing and becoming recognized as a specific job role. At IBM Nick joined what was initially the governance team, which became the IBM Cloud PAL team.

Approach

In the last eight years IBM has developed a design system to guide the consistent application of design elements across the IBM product set. Initially, the main design system, called Carbon, was not detailed enough to include all the different elements that could be used for products across the company as a whole. This is when IBM developed the Pattern and Asset Library (PAL). The PAL grew into the IBM Cloud PAL, a library of premade digital design components for teams working on the IBM Cloud platform. Nick explains, 'These pattern and asset libraries are used when an organization or a product zone needs more definition, because the full high-level-tier design system has become too abstract for any individual team to take and do things specifically with.' IBM found that lots of teams working on the IBM Cloud platform were creating solutions for the same problem, and this was not a good use of resources or time. Tessa and her team supported the implementation of the IBM Cloud PAL design system, making sure it was being applied in the right way; using constant engagement and feedback, the team continues to develop the system.

The IBM Cloud PAL helps to cut down on duplicated work by integrating software engineering with design components. Nick explains, 'If you have a developer on team A who creates a header component which has a ton of code built into it, teams B, C and D through Z can pick up that header and don't have to rewrite all the code.' Through the IBM Cloud PAL,

Layout grids and padding

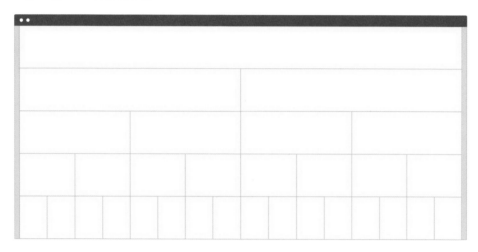

Colour values

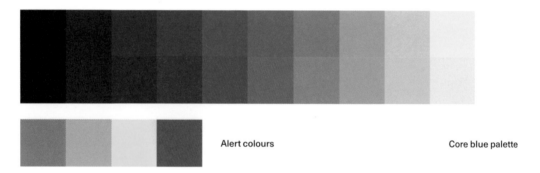

Alert colours   Core blue palette

Typography

Semibold (600)   *Semibold Italic (600)*

Regular (400)   *Italic (400)*

Light (300)   *Light Italic (300)*

The IBM Cloud PAL includes a range of precoded
elements that cover all aspects of visual design.

the role of designers is changing in teams, from being the bricklayers constructing the building to becoming the architects. This type of change in thinking helps designers understand business and play a key part in the successful development of a company.

Because of the wide role that a design system plays in a company, it is important that it has universal buy-in from all involved. Engaging all the teams that will be using it helps to create a valuable system that is consistently used. Tessa says that getting designers to 'focus on the whole design rather than details of each element (that have already been created) helps create a better all-round experience'. This gives teams the opportunity to ask bigger, fundamental questions rather than spending time on finer details: for example, if a form is needed at all, rather than the details of how a form works.

Nick explains that the aim of the design system was, paradoxically, to 'intentionally limit what teams can do, and in doing so actually enable them to do broader and bigger thinking'. 'Every day,' he says, 'the teams wanted to write a novel, yet they were trying to invent a language at the same time, and we're like, hey, we got the language for you, now you can go write your novel.' He says that we are at an 'inflection point in the industry, moving from a place where design teams work against each other on a product, trying to craft a better thing, to coming together to produce something that is repeatable, scalable and reusable'. This gives teams the opportunity to create better-quality products, because each element can be consistent and refined. Tessa adds, 'For example, for Ford to have the same gear shift in a Fiesta and a Focus is really good for the company. It's much more cost effective. If they are not wasting cycles on designing a gear shift, they may have more freedom to focus on safety, technological updates, and the form factor of the entire vehicle.' This shifts the designer's attention to the users and how to create the best possible experience.

Thoughts on the future

Nick and Tessa say that, while there will always be a need for skilled visual designers, the challenge is to close the gap between the designers and engineers. The disconnect between designers' and engineers' priorities creates a conflict. Nick goes on to say, 'I think design systems are the first real step towards design being a system that engineering can tap into, so that designers can do their craft, but when it goes to production and the engineers pick it up, the engineers now are doing far less translation work and they're getting to the point where a distinct link has been crafted seamlessly between design and engineering.'

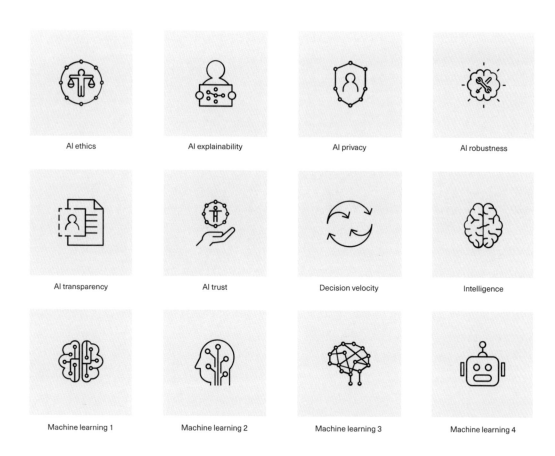

AI ethics	AI explainability	AI privacy	AI robustness
AI transparency	AI trust	Decision velocity	Intelligence
Machine learning 1	Machine learning 2	Machine learning 3	Machine learning 4

The IBM Cloud PAL also includes icons that can be deployed throughout a product.

This closing of the gap between designers and engineers, Nick and Tessa say, can be achieved through the design system, which allows designers to move from a focus on the micro details of the pixel approach to a macro workflow approach that enables designers to focus on users and their journey to create a faster iterative process. Tessa has begun to notice design systems developing from simple front-end components to components connected to microservices, guidance around conversational UX, AI ethics, and data collection considerations.

The design system is a complex organism that is constantly evolving and changing, but because of this it has endless potential to create real change, as long as everyone wants that change to happen.

1.3 Understanding the client

As a UX designer in a team, when you first begin to work with a client, understanding an account manager's brief and determining the client's requirements can be challenging. It is important to appreciate everyone's knowledge and skills and what they can bring to the team – including those of the client.

The client has come to work with the team you are part of because your team has a set of skills that is right for them and they are putting their trust in you to help them, but their specialist knowledge is equally important. The client's role and their relationship with the team you are part of is essential to producing a great outcome.

Part of working with a client is translating what is being asked of you into a design brief that can engage and energize a creative team to produce an exciting outcome. This can involve helping the client express the brief and then refine it further. It is important that you – collectively as a team, and individually as a UX designer – are clear on what the objectives of a project are, as well as the context of the project and how it sits within larger projects. You need to be

11 An important part of UX design is being able to understand and translate the objectives of a project.

| As proposed by the project sponsor | As specified in the project request | As designed by the senior analyst | As produced by the programmers | As installed at the user's site | What the user wanted |

sure that you understand what is being asked of you and be able to express this in a brief that the client can then agree to (fig. 11). Once this has been achieved, the brief becomes an overarching document that functions as both the starting point and an ongoing reference for a creative team.

What a client really means

The language of the UX design discipline is going to be different from the language of your clients, who are experts in their own field – the way they use certain words may conflict with how you interpret the same words, or may not give you the detail or inspiration you need to define a project. Sometimes the message becomes lost in translation. There are a number of different approaches that can help you, your team and your client overcome this.

First, make sure the project is structured with key milestones, which can be used as points at which the team and the client come together and check in on the project to make sure that everyone is on the same page. It is important to have a working document that covers an agreed statement of intent, set of requirements and design brief (see 'Writing a brief', p. 34).

Second, as you plan meetings, consider how to bring everyone together. A visual approach can be helpful to quickly communicate ideas and generate discussion. For example, if you tell a room of people that you would like to paint the room green, they could all be imagining different shades of green. The easiest way to make sure that they know the colour you are thinking of is to show them (fig. 12).

12 Sometimes the best way to clearly communicate ideas is to show people exactly what you mean: for example, by showing a range of colours rather than trying to describe shades of green.

Depending on what stage a project is at, there are a number of ways you can kickstart a meeting (fig. 13). For example, a card sort – where a participant is asked to arrange a set of cards containing words or pictures into different groups or orders of importance – is a good activity at the beginning of a project to narrow down ideas and thoughts and focus the team's direction. In early stages, it is good to encourage a wide-ranging conversation to help discover and explore ideas, using a broad set of visual sources that do not necessarily concentrate exclusively on digital products (e.g., architecture, graphics, art, films, animation, etc.). As a project progresses, meetings may come to focus more on example interactions of user journeys (see 'Storytelling', p. 87) and presentations of mock-ups (see 'High-fidelity mock-ups', p. 144).

Writing a brief

A brief that inspires and enthuses can give a creative team the freedom to produce concepts and ideas in the best possible way. Part of this is setting the parameters and defining the details of a brief in just the right way – you do not want to be too vague, but you also do not want to be so restrictive that there is no room for manoeuvre. You want your brief to inspire and to create excitement and engagement in order to generate ideas for a project. You can do this through words and visual elements, but pitching the brief in the right way is vital – when Michelangelo was commissioned to paint the ceiling of the Sistine

S	**Specific:** have a clear and well-defined goal
M	**Measurable:** have a way of showing you are making progress
A	**Attainable:** be ambitious but achievable
R	**Relevant:** align values and objectives
T	**Time-based:** have a deadline or key milestones

SMART GOALS

Chapel, he was not briefed to 'cover the cracks' but to 'paint our ceiling for the greater glory of God and as an inspiration and lesson to his people'. The two different briefs in this example have the potential to provoke very different responses. The brief should bring clarity and a starting point to any project, balancing helpful structure with enough freedom to ignite ideas.

The brief should always be created with the client. It should be an exciting and engaging part of the conversation that sets out the ambitions of the project while building trust and relationships with the client. It is important that you share the brief with clients and colleagues to get feedback, and be prepared to make a few changes to the brief as it develops. This way, all parties are engaged and you can begin to generate a form of contract.

A brief for a creative team brings together a number of elements in a single document. It is normally short – usually a single A4 or Letter page, no more than two. In a larger project, you might have briefs for each different element of the project. The brief should contain a statement about the problem to be solved, who the audience is, possible approaches and any mandatory requirements. The brief should also have a statement of ambition that communicates the aim of the project, and it should set SMART goals for the team (see above).

'Every great design begins with an even better story.'

Lorinda Mamo, designer

When discussing the target audience in a brief, make sure that you are describing how they feel and think. It is helpful to see the audience as a real person rather than a general concept. So instead of making a statement like 'Our male 30-to-40-year-old target hates arguing about breakfast with the kids', you could say 'Nick's head might explode if he has even one more battle with Isla and Harry about eating their cereal before school'. It is often through fun personas like this that you can really begin to discover who your target audience is. Create a real person, with a name, a job, hobbies, etc., that the team can keep in mind as they work on the concepts (for more on this, see 'Personas', p. 84).

Delivering a briefing

Writing a brief and delivering a briefing can be two very different experiences and require slightly different approaches. The briefing is much more experiential and interactive; it is not simply a case of reading out the written brief. The more fun and memorable the briefing is, the better. For example, if the target audience for the brief is about 'Nick, with two kids', consider giving the briefing in a family home, during breakfast (obviously in the next room!). Create mood boards showing the contents of Nick's cupboard, Nick's dreams, etc. Make an impact. Get the teams excited. Let them digest, ask questions. Check in with them the next day to see if they have any more questions. Inspire them to create!

You may find that, as a team, you need to refine the brief and revisit some of the key elements. If so, it is good practice to pick out keywords in the brief and use them to explore the true focus of the brief. As the project proceeds, the brief can be referred to at different points to make sure the project is on track. You can check your progress through creative reviews, feedback or informal meetings. As the design journey progresses and the project develops, the brief may be challenged and refined through continuous questioning and interrogation, research and contextualization of ideas.

The client and design relationship

Stacey McInnes has a breadth of experience working with clients and creative teams. She worked in advertising agencies in Toronto and New York, and was the head of strategic planning at Publicis before joining the start-up Cluep, an artificial intelligent mobile ad platform that targets people based on what they're sharing, how they're feeling and where they go in the physical world. At Cluep, Stacey is the chief operating officer, working with operations, technical and sales teams to make sure products meet clients' expectations.

Approach

Achieving the best possible outcome from a design process requires understanding the brand, defining the brand and articulating the vision of the brand that culminates in a core concept. Stacey says it is important to ask 'What is this brand trying to represent? Where is it trying to get from and where is it trying to go? And what does it need to represent in order to create powerful feelings and emotions and perceptions around that brand that are appropriate for it in this moment

and going forward generally?' To achieve this, Stacey's role at Publicis involved the rigorous analysis and foundational work needed to understand client requirements and turn them into a creative brief. Stacey describes this first stage as the 'extraction stage'. The brief then enables creative teams to generate a set of ideas and possibilities. At this point in the process, Stacey's role is to help the creative teams express their visual ideas in a way that the client will understand from a business perspective.

The first stage of working with a client, Stacey explains, is to discuss the process of the project. Stacey says it is important to 'define the process very clearly'. She goes on to explain, 'This analysis is quite rigorous, often involving an internal analysis that's going to involve the business/client' and also an external analysis of the landscape that the client operates in. (For more on this, see 'Understanding the user', p. 84.)

For the internal analysis, Stacey says, 'We need to meet the senior executives. There will be interviews, workshops, an audit of all the materials and a desire to understand where they're going and their vision.' Doing this 'pulls up the strengths of a company and their culture' and enables questions to be asked, such as 'Where do you see yourselves and the future of the competition?'

For the external analysis, a 'landscape audit' can help a client to understand forces that drive the company from outside. This might involve looking at industry papers, competitor activity, consumer behaviour and cultural drivers of society or the community. For a UX designer, this is also likely to involve user research and analysis to better understand how users currently interact with an existing product.

Undertaking both internal and external analysis helps to build a 360° view of the client and their market positioning, which in turn can give a strong indication of the direction the client needs to take. This also helps with setting out project timelines and key checkpoints along the way.

After time has been spent synthesizing and developing ideas, it is important to continue the conversation with the client, presenting findings back and using this as a basis for further discussion on how the brand might be being perceived and some of the themes that are already emerging. This enables the creation of a 'functional' storyline that helps teams to determine the 'jumping-off point'. Stacey explains that creating a storyline that encapsulates the key findings and has an overall direction enables the client to see the bigger picture. Stacey says, 'In the case of [humanitarian NGO] CARE, we did a piece of work with the core organization. But there are eight or nine member countries who are the ones on the ground. The member countries execute the programmes; they are the ones engaging with the real people, so their input and buy-in was critical.'

The CARE logo was developed through storytelling that helped the creative team understand what drives the organization.

'If brands are about relationships, you've always got to know who you are, what you are, what you want to be, and you have got to know your audience.'

She continues: 'For example, it was important to respect the member country needs and to make sure that we expressed the concept in a way that does not make the member countries feel poorly about the brand (CARE) that's supposed to be helping them – that would be horrible. So member countries would be involved up front as well, and all of that has to happen before we then sit down and brief the creative teams and really engage them in the process.'

In the next stage of the process, the creative team are briefed. Often at this point there is a rough framework to work within. Stacey says, 'Let's say we've got the brief. We kind of know the grounding of it, but we want to explore different territories and what they might mean. So, we might develop conceptual territories as either programme or brand spaces that might have a theme to help the creative team develop and explore ideas that they will push and pull with the main strategy team.' For example, 'When the creative teams come back to us with their ideas, they'll often link it back to the strategy: What components drove them? How did it come about?'

With CARE, Stacey says the creative team developed components and storylines based on the concept of the hands, explaining what they started with and why the concept worked. Then, Stacey says, 'the creative team will start to build a story. A lot of times they won't have the full story or they might only have the beginning of it, and then what we'll do is start to come back and say "That is amazing, yes, I understand the idea, now we'll help build you an even richer talk track". It will help the creative team express the story even more fully so that when we go to the client, they can't help but follow along, and when we arrive at the conclusion the client has already bought it.' Stacey says that with CARE the work involved shifting their storyline from sending supplies to self-empowerment and a way out of poverty.

Being able to tell stories and communicate an idea to make sure that everyone is on the same page is essential – being able to present concepts to the client, but also being able to inspire and brief creatives. Storytelling can be an enabler of change, and by generating understanding it can lead to a re-evaluation of the customer or audience and how to engage with them and inform how a product behaves.

All the different approaches and processes that enable the successful relationship with a client require constant team work from both sides, and this can be seen throughout the process that Stacey has discussed. This process of good communication and the importance of storytelling have been around for millennia and are not to be taken for granted. Strong skills in storytelling and collaborating are crucial to the success of any project.

Thoughts on the future

With such well-established processes, what might the future hold for client relationships and briefs? Stacey says, 'If brands are about relationships, you've always got to know who you are, what you are, what you want to be, and you have got to know your audience. The audience and landscape can be broad, or it can be individual. I don't see that part of the activity changing a whole lot because you still need to find that connection and you have got to find what's going to compel people and motivate them emotionally. There have been changes in the last 10 years that are going to continue. In the past, brands were more assertive, whereas more and more we've seen an embracing and engaging of people. Brands have continued to learn and organizations have learned to

be more responsive. Therefore, as the landscape changes and evolves, brands need to be continually fluid, in the sense of how they do things and how they engage more. This is by listening to the user and understanding that the conversation goes in two directions – something we have been talking about since digital came about. Publicis used the concept of "contagious ideas", the concept that these ideas build, and so you let others build your story for your brand. However, ultimately it is about creating a relationship and so both sides have to be involved and that doesn't change.'

A constantly changing digital landscape means constantly keeping an eye on the bigger picture. 'If you start with an open mind about what your brand stands for, and understand why you do what you do, what you really want to accomplish and what you care about, you will be able to stay true to your goals. But always with the understanding that the way that this is fulfilled could change over time.'

1.4 Multiplatform space

There are many different platforms – that is, media (singular, medium) – that you can use to engage with an audience: print, film, web, social media, billboards, newspapers, TV, movies, podcasts, etc. Users interact with and use them all differently, but everyone uses most of them in one way or another, so they should not be viewed in isolation but as a group of products that engage your audience in different ways. We are going to look at how they all work together and how you can use them effectively for a multiplatform campaign.

This section will look at different interactive environments – be they immersive, screen based or a hybrid of the two – and begin to look at how they work together and how they can be utilized to create multiplatform solutions that sit across a range of different media with a range of different audience demands. Even though we use many different devices each day, it is easy to become complacent about how we are interacting with them and the established conventions that we are using to do so. Yet it is important to remember that these forms of technology and communication are still relatively new, and how we use and engage with them is still being explored. We can build on existing conventions or use them in a fresh and engaging way.

'Home' (2014)

Holly Herndon is an electronic musician who composes on her laptop computer. 'For my debut album, *Movement*, I communicated an intimacy with my laptop. It is my instrument, memory, and window to most people that I love. It is my Home. Our relationships with these interconnected devices are still so young, so naive.'

Her song 'Home', from the album *Platform*, was inspired by revelations that spy agencies collect private data from citizens every day. She describes 'Home' as 'a break up song with the devices with which I shared a naive relationship'. The music video by Metahaven features a 'data rain' of symbols that represent private information that was never intended to be made public.

'As a culture, we are in a process of accelerated, and reluctant, maturation.'

Holly Herndon

Still image from the music video for Holly Herndon's song 'Home'.

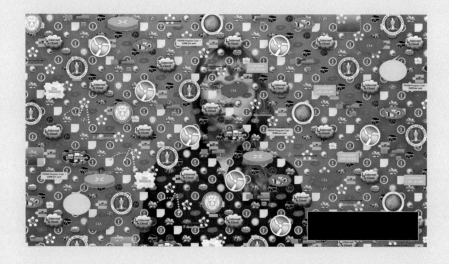

A digital platform can be broadly defined as a collection of technologies that delivers information to a user. Generally, digital platforms

- **Enable electronic communications**
- **Are displayed on a digital device**
- **Can often be used on demand – any time, anywhere**
- **Facilitate user interaction and participation in a way that 'old media' cannot**
- **Give users a different view or representation of the world.**

Digital platforms share many of the ideals of the internet, offering users the chance to

- **Be part of a community**
- **Share**
- **Have a voice**
- **Contribute**
- **Create value**
- **Generate content**
- **Enhance our experience of the world (both physical and virtual)**
- **Attain digital citizenship.**

Looking at the lists above, we can see that digital platforms are based in more than technology. As media theorist Marshall McLuhan says, electronic media change the way we live our lives and who we are. Martin Lister, a researcher and teacher of media studies, identifies the emergence of 'new media' as an 'epoch-making' phenomenon that is 'part of a much larger landscape of social, technological and cultural change; in short . . . part of a new technoculture'. When we think of multiplatform environments we need to think of the audience within that larger landscape, as well as considering what the platform and technology can offer us as UX designers.

14 The input –
compute – output
sequence.

Physical interactive spaces and immersive environments

When we think of a computer, we often first think of its component parts: screen, keyboard, mouse and processor. However, our interactions with the technology can be broken down into a basic sequence of input – compute – output (fig. 14). For example, when you type a letter on a keyboard (input), a signal is sent to the processor (compute) that then displays the letter on your screen (output).

This sequence can be applied to a multitude of other interactions. For example, you could have an input of a measurement from a thermometer and an output of a light, with the computer programmed to turn the light on when the room reaches a certain temperature. You could use a similar computer interaction to change the speed of a fan based on the popularity of a hashtag on a social media platform.

By thinking in terms of inputs and outputs, you can begin to look beyond screen-based interactions and create immersive environments that users can interact with using a range of senses. There are many different approaches to creating interactive immersive, and often playable, environments (figs 15–25). Though some of these projects use a physical space as well as a digital one, the underlying process of creation and approach is not necessarily any different. The focus is still on understanding and interacting with an audience or users. Use the principle of input – compute – output to break down and explore a concept or an idea. Free your mind and don't let yourself be limited by what you already know is possible. Sometimes what might at first seem complicated can be quite simple to create.

GALLERY – PAGE 49

Different platforms, same experience

A good campaign will engage an audience across different platforms. This is true whether you're working on a single campaign or an ongoing form of community engagement. Online dating app Tinder and advertising agency 72andSunny used a multiplatform approach to create an interactive event called Swipe Night, where Tinder members were taken on a choose-your-own-adventure journey where the choices they made helped to determine who they were matched with. The event ran as a series of five-minute episodes within the Tinder app, but it was also publicized on Twitter and generated mainstream media interest.

GALLERY – PAGE 55

Thinx, a company that makes menstrual underwear, and BBDO New York created a multiplatform solution for an advertising campaign designed to break taboos about talking about menstruation (fig. 25). The advertisement, in which a boy tells his father he has his first period, was rejected by many media outlets in the United States, but this was then used as a jumping-off point to raise the issue on chat shows and other outlets. Eventually the advertisement was allowed to be aired, and it then generated an active conversation on social media.

Make sure that you are creating considered campaigns that sit across a number of different platforms, because it is too simplistic to think that people just use one platform and nothing else. To be part of a community and engage your audience, it is important to ensure your campaigns have a presence across a range of appropriate platforms.

Same platforms, different experience

Even when your audience is using the same platform, it is an over-simplification to assume that all users will interact with your creations in the same way. Therefore, it is necessary to understand who your audience are, and how, where and when they are going to interact with your product.

Danah Boyd highlights the difference in audience engagement and use in her book *It's Complicated: The Social Lives of Networked Teens*. A teen whose only access to the internet is through a library computer and one who has their own internet-capable devices will use social media very differently. The more people use and interact with a platform, the more they become familiar with the intricacies of the platform and the etiquette of how to use it; they learn the 'critical knowledge to engage productively'. Meanwhile, those whose access is less frequent are less thoroughly able to explain how the platform works, and they do not have the extra depth of interaction that is acquired through integrating the platform into their lives.

For this reason, it is important to understand that how you interact with technology is not always the same as how others will interact with it. Historian of technology Melvin Kranzberg says, 'Technology is neither good nor bad; nor is it neutral.' Platforms have a bias towards whoever has created them, and it takes a great deal of understanding and empathy to create solutions that are not made for the creator themselves.

This is not entirely bad; technology does create opportunity and possibility, but, as science fiction writer William Gibson says, 'The future is already here – it's just not very evenly distributed.' Keep this in mind when creating products and solutions, and when exploring the opportunities offered by different platforms. The quality of a user's experience and the external factors affecting their experience are intrinsically linked.

It is also worth considering the technology you are using itself. As a UX designer, you are both a creator and user of technology and in turn can affect change in a positive way. Approaching UX design with a social conscience will help you create solutions for a much broader audience, and not just for you and your friends.

Part 1

Summary

This section has introduced the digital design process and given you a good foundation for creating screen-based digital solutions. Now that you understand some of the different approaches to creating solutions, you can make informed decisions on the possible design journey you might embark on in a project, being mindful of how to collaborate with a range of people from different disciplines to steer the project to a successful outcome.

By keeping in mind the importance of thinking about your audience and who you are creating content for, as well as some of the benefits and challenges of using different platforms, you can create solutions that begin to move beyond screen-based designs and into interactive and immersive spaces. Remember Don Norman's definition of UX as 'everything . . . and how you experience it'.

Gallery 1.4: Multiplatform space

15 Dominic Wilcox's *No Place Like Home* GPS shoes (2012)
incorporate useful wayfinding technology in an unusual platform.

16 Rafael Lozano-Hemmer's *Remote Pulse* (2019) is an interactive installation that allows people to feel each other's heartbeat, using two terminals – one in El Paso, Texas, and the other in Ciudad Juárez, Chihuahua – connected by the internet to bring people together across the US–Mexico border. Originally presented as part of the public art installation *Border Tuner/ Sintonizador Fronterizo* by Rafael Lozano-Hemmer at Bowie High School, El Paso, and Parque Chamizal, Ciudad Juárez.

TOP RIGHT **17** *Topologies #1* (2020), by United Visual Artists, explores viewers' perceptions and relationship with space, using five moving sculptures that project light to constantly reshape a room. The work was originally commissioned by Nxt Museum, the first museum dedicated to new media art in the Netherlands.

BOTTOM RIGHT **18** Jacquard by Google is the first full-scale digital technology platform created to incorporate personalized digital experiences and services into apparel, footwear and other everyday essentials. Answer phone calls from your jacket sleeve, or get directions from your backpack.

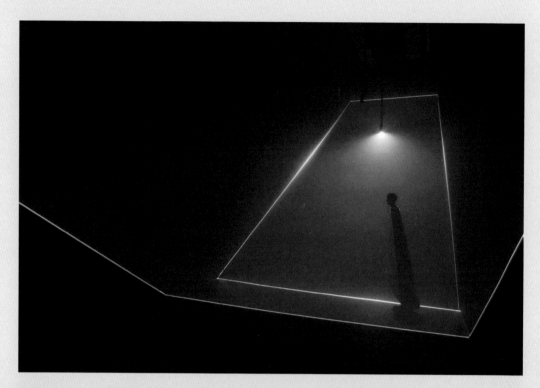

19 *Baloica* (2013) by Elas Duas is an interactive sound installation that transforms a swing set into a musical instrument. A motion sensor captures the movements of people on the swings as they rock back and forth, triggering different sounds. The more people on the swings, the more complex the music becomes.

20 Three-dimensional virtual versions of sculptures by artist Jeff Koons, including his *Balloon Dog*, were exhibited in nine international cities, visible only via the Snapchat smartphone app. Artist Sebastian Errazuriz protested the exhibition by creating a vandalized replica of Koons's artwork and displaying it virtually in Central Park, New York.

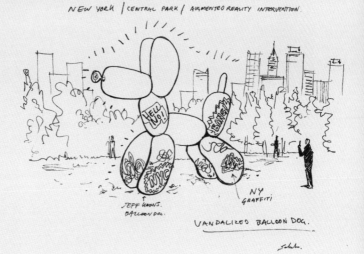

NEW YORK | CENTRAL PARK | AUGMENTED REALITY INTERVENTION.

JEFF KOONS.
BALLOON DOG.

NY
GRAFFITI

VANDALIZED BALLOON DOG.

RIGHT   21 Sketch by Sebastian Errazuriz of his planned protest against Koons's *Balloon Dog*.

22 Olafur Eliasson's *Wunderkammer* (2020), supported by Acute Art, uses augmented reality to render a variety of objects and natural phenomena from Eliasson's studio, allowing viewers to add these objects to their personal spaces. The collection includes a raincloud, a solar lantern that is charged by an AR sun, and animals such as a puffin and an insect.

23 *Webs of Life* (begun in 2020) is an augmented reality project by Tomás Saraceno with Arachnophilia that attempts to connect the digital and physical worlds. Viewers gain access to Saraceno's virtual spider by photographing a real spider in the natural world and uploading it to an app. Installation view of *Maratus speciosus*, presented as part of 'Back to Earth' at the Serpentine Galleries, London, 2021, curated by Rebecca Lewin. Project supported by Acute Art.

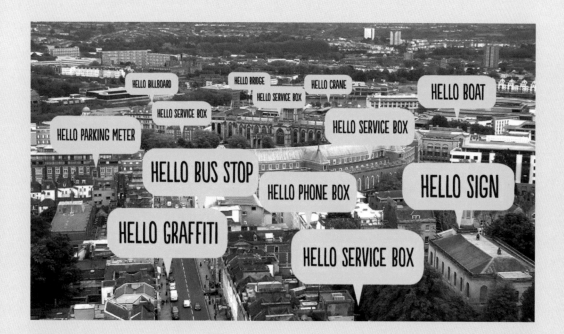

24 PAN Studio created Hello Lamp Post, an interactive messaging platform that allows people to have conversations with street objects – lamp posts, parking meters, etc. – around their city using the text message app on their phone.

25 The 'MENstruation' advertising campaign for Thinx by BBDO New York used a range of platforms as well as television to communicate its message.

knowing your audience

2.1 **Data collection**

Collecting data is a valuable part of getting to know your audience. Data collection happens every day on nearly every platform in the digital world. Understanding the power of data – how to collect it, analyze it, present it and use it to inform projects and campaigns – is essential to the design process. If you are able to understand your audience, then you are able to create informed solutions tailored to that audience.

Anthropologist Daniel Miller talks about 'trapping' the audience by catching their interest: 'The Internet is best seen not as technology but as a platform which enables people to create technologies, and these in turn are designed for particular functions. So what people weave from the fibres of the Internet are the traps they use to catch particular kinds of passing surfer. They require a design that draws interest.' He gives an example of Trinidadian wholesalers' websites, which were particularly ugly and not something that attracted consumers, but the target audience saw them as functional and approved of the wholesaler not wasting money on unnecessary 'design'.

Interviews are another way to gain valuable data to help you understand your audience, but they must be undertaken in a way that is going to give truly meaningful information. For example, Caroline Criado Perez in her book *Invisible Women* points out that women are the primary users of public transport systems and make multiple journeys for multiple reasons, yet most interviews gathering data on transport use do not include the necessary questions to extract this information, and any that do put a lower priority on the journeys that women are likely to make. If you don't understand the needs of your users, you cannot create a system that is right for them.

This data can then be used to create user journeys and user profiles, which help you think about your users as real people with lives that go beyond their interaction with your platform, people who are more than just the data that you have in front of you. Storytelling also plays a role in the creative process to help you understand your audience and your product. Build a more detailed picture of your users and you can create more meaningful interactions with them. Testing your product with real-world users at different stages of the design process gives you further important data to fine-tune your product.

Quantitative and qualitative data

There are two basic types of data: *quantitative* (measurable – e.g., a count of how many people visited your website) and *qualitative* (descriptive – e.g., a personal response to an interview question).

The type of data that is most often collected online is quantitative and gives us broad overviews of how users interact with online platforms. Examples of quantitative data are surveys, website visits and censuses. Every day we create digital contact points through our use of technology. Many of these contact points are recorded, generating little packets of quantitative information that, for example, might help a platform better understand their users to, in turn, help them improve their product. These can give us large datasets that can be used to identify statistical narratives, though you may need to focus on your key audience and filter your data in order to gain any meaningful insights.

Alongside this sits qualitative data, gathered in small datasets that are used to gain a quality of information that cannot often be gained from large datasets. Interviews, focus groups and observations are examples of qualitative data. Qualitative approaches often help us

You got this ad because you're a newlywed pilates instructor and you're cartoon crazy.

This ad used your location to see you're in La Jolla.

You're into parenting blogs and thinking about LGBTQ adoption.

26 A banned ad that instant messaging service Signal tried to use to highlight how companies like Facebook collect data about their users for use in advertising.

identify themes and experiences from individuals that may not be evident in a large impersonal quantitative dataset. Data should be collected ethically and with consent, although some companies obtain it less transparently by tracking their users online (fig. 26).

User interviews

Interviews are a qualitative approach that can help you to identify themes and experiences from individuals rather than from large pools of quantitative data. *Formal interviews* have a rigid structure and an agreed set of questions, which allow you to collect data that you can then compare with other participants. *Semi-structured interviews* have a rough set of questions or topics to cover but are much more conversational and informal, allowing you the possibility of exploring any unexpected information or themes that may emerge. Interviews do not need to be always conducted on a one-to-one basis – group interviews or focus groups are often appropriate and enable participants to share their experiences.

Interview activities

An interview does not always need to consist of you asking questions and the participant answering them. There are a number of approaches that you can take in order to gather different types of information. By asking participants to undertake a task – such as drawing, creating collages, card sorting or keeping a journal – you may be able to collect richer, more meaningful data than you might get from direct questioning. For example, if you were to ask 'When do you use technology during your week?' this could elicit answers such as 'All the time' or 'Occasionally', but having the participant map out their week and when they are likely to use technology can give you a much more in-depth response that will generate further discussion and conversation.

27 Card-sorting activities can help you identify your users' priorities.

Card-sorting activities: These are often valuable in working out what is important to a participant (fig. 27). The cards might contain a series of images or text or both that you ask the participant to put into groups or order by a particular priority. Card sorting can be a collaborative or an individual activity.

Journals: Asking your participant to keep a journal is a valuable way of collecting data prior to an interview. Specific tasks or activities could be recorded in a written journal or a photo journal.

28 Once your user interviews are complete, data mapping can help you identify relevant themes and issues in the qualitative data you have gathered.

Making or design activities: These can also be used to gather information more informally and conversationally from participants. Whatever route you take it is about working out the most appropriate way to get meaningful data for your project.

Where to conduct interviews

Where you conduct your interviews is important. Make sure that you have a space that is appropriate for any activities you may have prepared, and ensure that your participant is as comfortable as possible.

Depending on who you are interviewing, you may wish to allow the interviewee to choose where you meet, as this is likely to make them more comfortable in speaking to you and also gives you the opportunity to observe other behaviours or habits during the interview. Public spaces such as local community centres or cafés are often good places to meet, but you may also conduct an interview in the participant's home – if you do this, make sure that both you and the interviewee will be safe.

Conducting interviews via telephone or video calls is often ideal if you are working with participants that are geographically dispersed, but be aware that the type of interaction and information that you gather may be influenced by the medium you are using.

Once you have collected your qualitative data, the next step is to analyze the information you have gathered to identify common themes and ideas that you can then use to inform your next steps in your project, whether you are at the very beginning or investigating a particular stage of a user journey, or to measure the success of a campaign or a set of changes you are planning to implement (fig. 28).

2.2 Data analysis

Raw data on its own is not of any great use. Only when it is linked with other data does it gain meaning and become information. This, in turn, gives way to knowledge – an appropriate and focused collection of information – which, when applied, leads to wisdom.

This Data–Information–Knowledge–Wisdom hierarchy – often visualized as a data wisdom pyramid, associated with the organizational theorist Russell L. Ackoff – highlights the relationship between these different elements (fig. 29). For example, a list of words or letters (data) can be linked together to form words, sentences and paragraphs (information). These paragraphs can be organized into larger collections of focused information from a range of sources (knowledge), which can then be applied in various situations (wisdom).

Data analysis involves the collection and analysis of data to produce information that you can use to learn how people use your product and make decisions about the best way to improve your product.

There are different approaches to data analysis, and each has a slightly different emphasis.

Descriptive: uses data based on past events. It does not aim to explain why the data may present particular results; it reports the findings and nothing more.

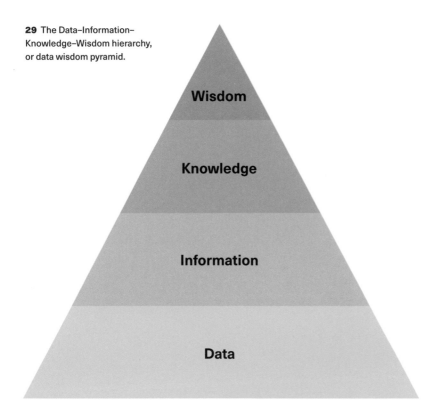

29 The Data–Information–Knowledge–Wisdom hierarchy, or data wisdom pyramid.

Wisdom

Knowledge

Information

Data

Diagnostic: helps you identify why particular results may be the case – for example, why you might have lots of hits on a web shop but not many people buying.

Predictive: uses patterns and trends in collected data to inform a possible future – for example, sales were not so high during the last summer, so you use this information to create a campaign to increase sales.

Prescriptive: reveals the best course of action. This analytical approach uses a combination of all the above: it seeks to understand what has happened (descriptive), and why (diagnostic), and then plan for the future (predictive). Prescriptive approaches are complicated as they require a lot of analysis and combination of different data sources.

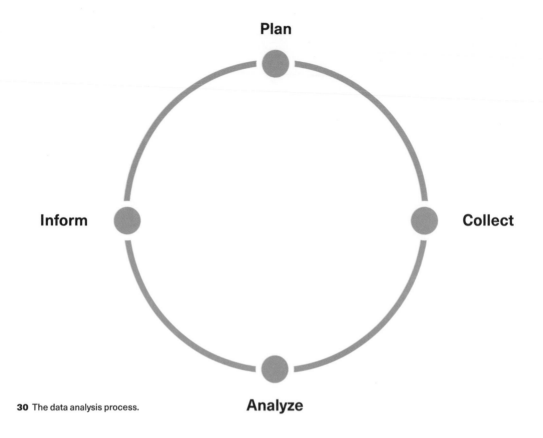

Plan

Inform

Collect

Analyze

30 The data analysis process.

There are four distinct stages in data analysis processes, which are essentially cyclical (fig. 30). Each stage informs the others.

1. Plan: Consider what you are trying to find out. Work out what your objectives are – this is not about a preconceived idea of what your results will be, but rather a question about your users or their behaviours. This will help you decide how to group the data you will collect.

2. Collect: How are you going to collect the data? For example, this could be through a survey or website. Once you know this, identify what it is that you are going to collect. It could be customer behaviours, customer affinities, or even failed searches for a product that you do not stock to help inform what you might want to stock in the future.

3. Analyze: Once you have data, how you organize and analyze it will have an impact on how you perceive the results. Often the first part of this stage brings together data from a range of sources, which is then filtered or segmented to create meaningful results – for example, identifying results from a specific demographic (more on this in the 'User testing' case study, p. 100).

4. Inform: The results of your data analysis should give you useful information that can inform decisions. How you visualize and present the data will play a key part in this.

There are a number of methods for analyzing data, and which one you use will depend on the type of dataset that you have. For example, qualitative data is not going to be easily converted to a series of graphs, and quantitative data is not going to suit thematic analysis.

Thematic analysis is a good approach for qualitative data, such as user interviews. This enables you to find recurring themes in different sets of data and identify important elements within the data. You can then group content into recurring categories, which can help you decide what is important and how a project can move forwards.

Affinity mapping

Affinity mapping is one particular approach to thematic analysis (fig. 31). Affinity mapping is undertaken as a group and is designed for interpreting data that has been gathered through activities such as user interviews, focus sessions and research sessions. The group will often start with coloured sticky notes (normally a different colour is used for each different data source, such as each individual inter-viewee), marker pens and data. Individually, they will identify common themes and issues, then come together, put their sticky notes on a large wall and work together to group the notes into common catego-ries or sub-categories. The data can be collated and shared within the group, using either a spreadsheet or photos. The group is then able to identify what the priorities are and what needs to be worked on.

Quantitative data is analyzed to compare two or more datasets: for example, the results of A/B testing (see 'A/B testing', p. 96) or comparing different products. In a similar way to qualitative data, quantitative data can be used to help inform what areas of a product should be given priority in the development process. Note that, when comparing quantitative datasets, you need to make sure that there is a significant statistical difference between the results, and that if you were to repeat the tests you would get the same results.

31 Affinity mapping can help you identify and analyze themes in your qualitative data.

'The goal is to turn data into information and information into insight.'

Carly Fiorina, business leader

2.3 Presenting data visually

Turning raw data into meaningful and valuable information requires skill and understanding. Data visualization is part of this process. Knowing different methods will enable you to present what is often complex information clearly and effectively.

Once you have a dataset, how you present your data to communicate your findings can have a dramatic impact and reveal information that cannot be shown through tables and numbers alone. Visualizations can communicate a clear and concise message quickly to a broad audience. The power of data visualization is something that has evolved particularly over the last 200 years. For example, in 1900 the sociologist and civil rights activist W. E. B. Du Bois and his team created a series of charts for the Exposition Universelle in Paris to demonstrate African American achievements and illustrate the lived experience of African Americans. In 1854 physician John Snow's mapping of data on a cholera outbreak in London helped identify that the spread of disease was clearly related to water pumps. During the Crimean War, Florence Nightingale used a coxcomb diagram to make a compelling case for better practices to save lives (figs 34–36).

GALLERY – PAGE 76

There are many different ways to present data for different reasons. Designer Stefanie Posavec says that the main functions of data visualization are to explain, to explore or to exhibit (figs 37–39). Each of the three require different approaches.

GALLERY – PAGE 78

ISOTYPE (1920s)

Otto and Marie Neurath along with Gerd Arntz developed a visual system called ISOTYPE (International System Of TYpographic Picture Education) to display complex data. The system uses symbols to represent a set quantity by assigning a value to each symbol and then repeating this as required. This system is widely used in many fields to represent data.

'To remember simplified pictures is better than to forget accurate numbers.'

Otto Neurath

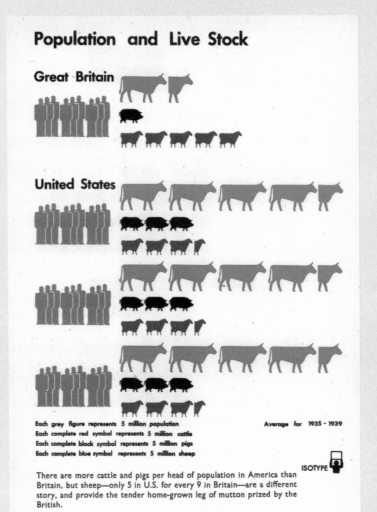

ISOTYPE chart produced by the Isotype Institute: 'Population and livestock', from Lella Secor Florence, *Only an Ocean Between* (London: Harrap, 1943). The Isotype Institute was founded by Otto and Marie Neurath.

Using the right type of visualization approach is important not only for representing your data most effectively, but also for engaging your intended audience. For example, how long will your audience be viewing the visualization and where will they be looking at it? If you know this and your intended message, you can then consider the best way to present your data and the story that the data can tell.

Structuring data with LATCH

Before you can choose your visualization approach, working out the best way to structure your data is vital to the success of communicating your message and helping people navigate your product (see also 'Structuring content', p. 130). Richard Saul Wurman developed LATCH as a guide to structuring, navigating and intersecting data (see below).

How you choose to structure your data will depend on your audience and the task at hand, as each display approach will yield different results. It is also worth carefully considering if the way in which you are structuring your data is reinforcing existing social structures, and if this is appropriate or not.

L A T C H	
L	**Location:** good for wayfinding, such as maps
A	**Alphabetical:** non-linear, such as a dictionary
T	**Time:** chronological, such as a step-by-step guide or a timetable
C	**Category:** similarities and relationships, such as how artworks are organized in a gallery
H	**Hierarchy:** from important to least important, such as most expensive to least expensive

You don't have to use just one LATCH approach at a time. For example, you could use *category* and *hierarchy* together to show similar items from the same category but arranged from most expensive to least expensive. Combining different structures helps you and your audience navigate complex datasets in valuable ways. Importantly, Wurman says, 'understanding the structure and organization of information permits you to extract value and significance from it'.

Types of visualizations

With data presentation, the details of how you communicate your information are also important. The choice of graph, map, image or other format, the colours used, the sizes and emphasis of different elements all have an impact on the way data tells a story. This is linked to the type of information that you are presenting. Ask yourself: Is the information location based, time based, or focused on relationships and connections? Does it have a hierarchy?

Using the appropriate visual to represent your data can make a great difference to how the data is interpreted. Cognitive neuroscientist Stephen Kosslyn, who looks at how we comprehend and perceive information, says that whatever form of presentation you choose to take, it is essential to keep the information

- Simple
- Relevant
- Appropriate
- Clearly defined
- Distinguished
- Conforming to expected conventions
- Salient and focused so as not to overwhelm the reader.

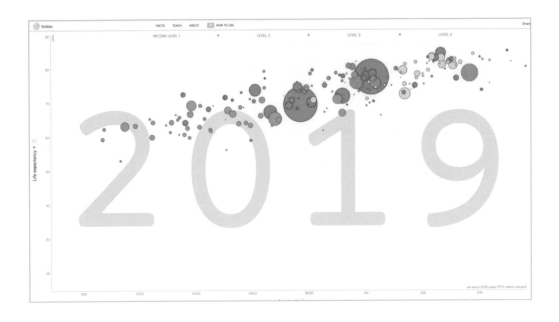

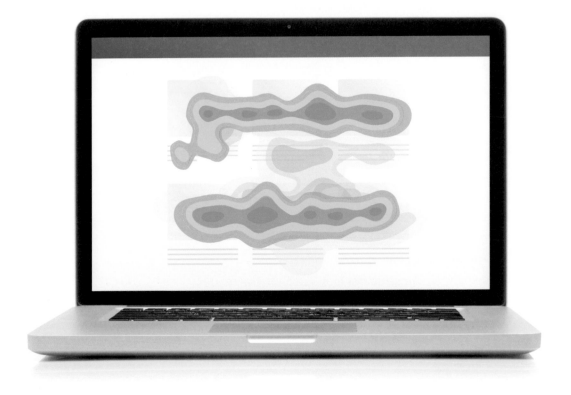

Per Mollerup, a Danish designer, academic and author who specializes in design simplicity, identifies three different types of visualization based on the type of information they present:

- **Quantities:** e.g., pie charts, bar charts, bubble charts (fig. 32), heat maps (fig. 33), picture tables
- **Locations:** e.g., scale maps, chorochromatic maps, dot distribution maps
- **Connections:** e.g., tree diagrams, mind maps, Venn diagrams, Euler diagrams, flow charts.

Storytelling with data

Knowing the ways that you can structure and visualize data gives you the skills to be able to present information, but the data is only of value if you can then use it to tell a story. Creating a narrative from your data, a story that has a beginning, middle and end, along with conflict and tension, is essential in engaging your audience. Cole Nussbaumer Knaflic outlines this process in her book *Storytelling with Data*, saying, 'Stories are magical. They have the power of captivating us and sticking with us in ways that facts alone cannot.'

Knaflic says that, along with a narrative and a story, you need to make sure you

- **Give context:** answer the questions Who?, What? and How? – Who is the story for? What is your story or goal? How are you going to show this?
- **Use appropriate visuals:** take your audience through a story – is a series of data visuals better than just one?
- **Eliminate clutter:** keep the message clear and direct (see 'Principles of design', p. 110).
- **Draw attention to the key part of your visual:** make sure your audience is focused on the data that helps explain the story you are telling.

32 A bubble chart uses bubbles of different sizes on a scatter plot to visualize data about life expectancy across different countries.

33 A heat map uses different colours to visualize the amount of attention users give to different parts of a webpage.

34 The stark black area in this graph represents the proportion of African Americans who were enslaved from 1790 to the 1860s compared to those who were free (in green). From a series of visualizations on African American progress by sociologist and civil rights activist W. E. B. DuBois for the 1900 Paris Exposition.

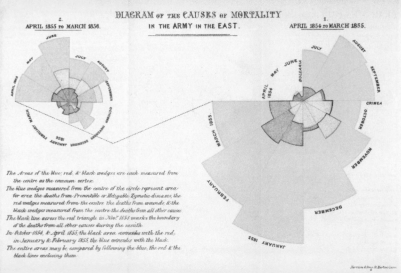

TOP **35** Dr John Snow used a dot distribution map to visualize a cholera outbreak in London in 1854.

BOTTOM **36** Florence Nightingale's coxcomb diagram effectively presented information about causes of death in the Crimean War in 1854–55. Blue represents deaths from preventable diseases; red, deaths from wounds; and black, deaths from all other causes.

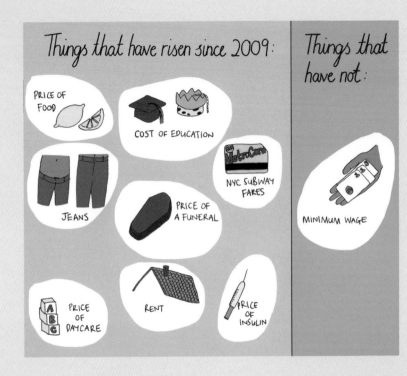

Things that have risen since 2009:

PRICE OF FOOD

COST OF EDUCATION

JEANS

PRICE OF A FUNERAL

NYC SUBWAY FARES

PRICE OF DAYCARE

RENT

PRICE OF INSULIN

Things that have not:

MINIMUM WAGE

LEFT **37** Mona Chalabi, 'Things That Have Risen Since 2009 – Things That Have Not'. Chalabi's work employs an engaging lo-fi hand-drawn aesthetic to convey data on often serious topics – in this case economics.

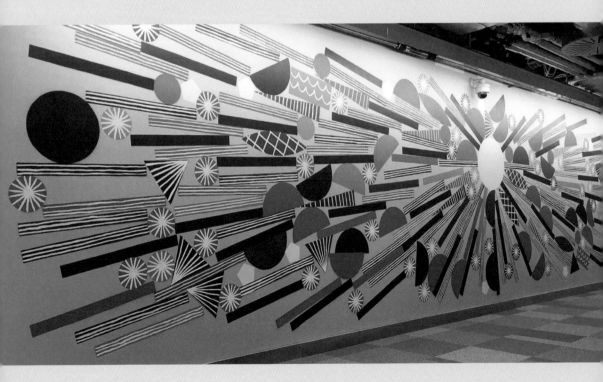

the
Average Colors of
Africa
per satellite imagery from Sentinel-2

more at erdavis.com

LEFT **38** A mural by Stefanie Posavec (2015), loosely visualizing data from a very long Facebook post, created (with The Mural Artists) for Facebook's London campus through their artist-in-residence programme.

39 A chorochromatic map by Erin Davis showing the average colour of different countries in Africa based on satellite imagery.

Communicating data

Stefanie Posavec is a designer, artist and author. In her design practice she explores new and experimental approaches to visualizing data and communicating information.

She has been a data-artist-in-residence with a range of organizations, from big tech companies such as Facebook to the National Maritime Museum in Greenwich, London. She has exhibited her work at museums and galleries around the world, including the Museum of Modern Art, New York, where her work is also in the permanent collection; the Storefront for Art and Architecture, New York; the Centre Pompidou, Paris; ArtScience Museum, Singapore; and the Victoria and Albert Museum, Design Museum, Wellcome Collection, Science Museum, Southbank Centre, and Somerset House, London.

Stefanie sees data visualization as being important because it makes data accessible: 'It is a way of opening up data to a wider audience and making data more memorable, but also it enables researchers to discover patterns that you might not notice within the data.' Stefanie does not use design programs or code; rather, she works with data in a variety of ways, such as using it to communicate insights, as in her book *Dear Data*, or to inform a design aesthetic. Stefanie does not describe herself as a data scientist or statistician, though she will often collaborate with a data scientist or statistician if she is working on a project that requires rigorous analysis or to bring multiple and complex data together.

Stefanie uses data 'as a material like other people might use clay or a pencil to communicate and share ideas with'. For example, she says, 'you might write a paragraph or take a photo to visualize a plant's data, but each way will offer something that the others don't, so you need to have as many tools as possible to understand the world around us'.

Approach

Stefanie's approach is to ask questions and to gather data in different ways: she might be given a dataset or a more traditional brief, or she might collect data of her own. She will then manually identify sets of information that guide her project's aesthetic. Once Stefanie has data, her next step is to analyze

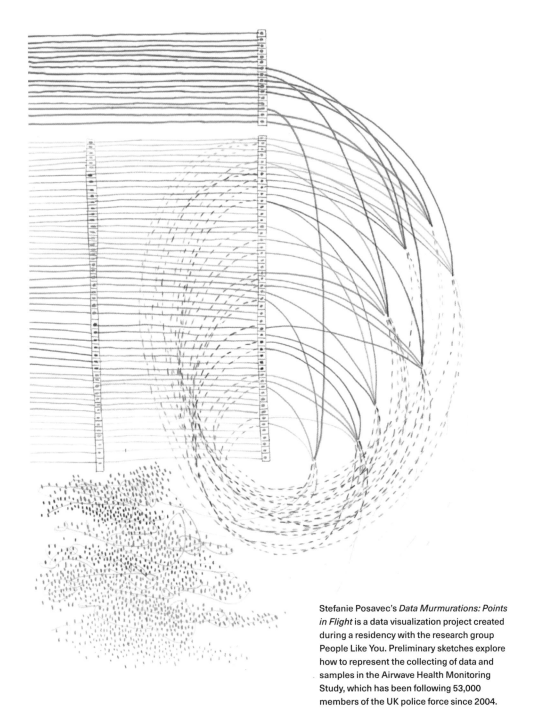

Stefanie Posavec's *Data Murmurations: Points in Flight* is a data visualization project created during a residency with the research group People Like You. Preliminary sketches explore how to represent the collecting of data and samples in the Airwave Health Monitoring Study, which has been following 53,000 members of the UK police force since 2004.

'Data visualization is a way of opening up data to a wider audience and making data more memorable.'

it to see what is interesting and relevant to help communicate her intended message, whether there are any outliers or anything strange in the data, what categories or data types there might be, and if there is anything that might be tricky to design a visualization for. She will then consider in more detail where and how the visualization is going to be viewed and who the audience is: 'a visualization in a PowerPoint may have limited viewing time, while people in a gallery are going to spend longer and in a different way.' Stefanie then starts to develop her concepts. First, she sketches on paper,

which enables her 'not to be constrained by visualization software or design software'. Only after this initial sketching of ideas does she move on to a computer.

When Stefanie took up a residency with the data science stream of People Like You, she was able to use her visualization skills to offer a different perspective on how the various stakeholders in a biobank perceive the 'people behind the numbers' who consent to their biological samples and data being used and stored for research. Stefanie was able to help give direction to more rigorous research.

Stefanie's main dataset was from the Airwave Health Monitoring Study, a cohort study and biobank based at the School of Public Health at Imperial College London, which has been following 53,000 members of the police force since 2004 to investigate whether the Airwave communication system used by the police has any long-term effects on their health. As well as using the dataset, Stefanie also used interviews and research to give further depth to her understanding of the study process as a whole.

Her visualization brought together a range of data that was previously separate, which enabled the study team to understand

Stefanie Posavec, *Data Murmurations: Points in Flight*, in-progress sketches visualizing data collection in the Airwave Health Monitoring Study.

and explain the process in a new way. This in turn offered a reflective talking point for many different groups: the team running the Airwave study, research groups and the wider research community. This has allowed the study team to make the work that they do more visible.

Thoughts on the future

Despite the fact that companies often do not share their data, data collection proliferates and data visualization has become particularly popular in the last 10 years. For these reasons, Stefanie hopes that data will be less 'siloed' in the future and become a key part of every designer's toolkit.

From a data visualization perspective, Stefanie is excited to move beyond static charts and storytelling to things such as a '3D virtual space or augmented reality, where you might see data in a space or hear it on your headphones'. Using new and emerging spaces opens up the opportunity to experience data in different ways.

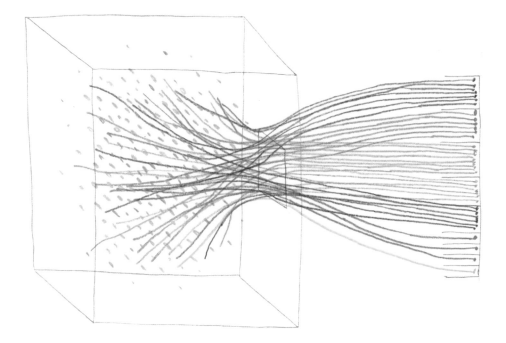

2.4 Understanding the user

Understanding your audience is essential to creating solutions that are fresh, compelling and appropriate for users. For example, a website for 80-year-old roller skaters requires a very different approach to a website for a K-pop band. Creating personas and mapping user journeys are effective ways to get to know your users in more detail (we looked briefly at personas in 'Writing a brief', p. 34).

These approaches build on human-centred design methods as a way to include users in co-designed pieces of work, and use storytelling as a way to understand and empathize with the user. This section will help answer some of the following fundamental questions:

- Who is your audience?
- Why will they be using your product?
- What is a user going to want from your product?
- How can you appeal to them?
- How much time will they have?
- How will they be viewing the work?
- Where are they going to be viewing your product?

Personas

A persona is an imagined user of your product, created from details acquired through research and data analysis (fig. 40). Your research might include talking to people one to one or in focus groups, through

FREELANCE FRANCESCA

DEMOGRAPHICS

Freelance marketing coordinator
Married
40
Gen X
Spanish
No kids yet but she has a dog and a cat
University master's degree
€60,000/year
Madrid, Spain

GOALS & NEEDS

- She wants to work more independently in environments that inspire her.
- She needs a space that is comfortable and convenient but also is in and around people and/or nature.
- She wants to be able to work freely from places that inspire her; this is where her best creative productivity happens.

HOBBIES & INTERESTS

She loves trying new restaurants and cafes, discovering and learning about new food and cultures, hiking, swimming, bike riding, going for walks, travelling, camping, interacting with friends and family, meeting new people, yoga.

USAGE & BENEFITS VARIABLES

Benefits: how to combine work and being outside?How to be able to change environment to work in to help boost/inspire creativity? How can I make meetings/working remotely interesting?
Usage: pay-per-use (instead of membership fee) is ideal for her as her lifestyle changes frequently and she likes to be spontaneous.
Volume purchase: she probably will use something like this an average of 5x/month.
Price sensitivity: she is fairly money-conscious since she already pays member-ship fees for other products and services for her work and she continues to invest in furthering her education also.

SOCIAL CHANNELS

CHARACTERISTICS

Fun-loving, easy-going, mindful, loving, compassionate, thoughtful, considerate, empathetic, loyal and adventurous

Extroverted Introvert

DREAMS & ASPIRATIONS

She dreams of complete financial freedom, time freedom, being debt-free, the ability to buy a house with her own outdoor space one day.

MOTIVATORS

- She likes the buzz of public-space working (the energy of people going about their day, not feeling alone, enjoying the weather/sun/fresh air, a reason to go outside/leave the house).
- As an early majority adopter, she likes to try new things but prefers the safety of a free trial period before committing, also often prefers pay-as-you-go options to term plans.

PAIN POINTS

- She never seems to have enough time/freedom to spend as much time as she likes outside.
- Doesn't have a suitable outdoor space of her own.
- Doesn't have/can't go to a physical office so she doesn't have 'anywhere to go' (which sometimes leaves her feeling isolated).
- She likes to be around people and civilization when she's working (which doesn't happen at home).
- She likes working in co-working spaces, cafes and restaurants, but not all the time as they can be too costly or busy.
- There aren't many places one can go to work outside (like in a park) that have everything one would need (plug in, shelter, wifi/reception, table and chair).
- She doesn't have good data reception sometimes so she needs wifi.

BIO

Francesca lives in a two-bedroom apartment with her husband and their cat and dog in a trendy area of Madrid, where they do not have an outdoor space of their own. She is within walking and/or bike-riding distance to many public services and parks, which they love as she enjoys being outside and goes for at least two walks per day with her dog (and sometimes her cat!). She does not have kids yet as they are newly married. Francesca spent her 20s travelling, her 30s schooling up and building her career success and is only just starting to get into thinking about kids. Her husband is a software engineer, and so they both freelance and work from home. She loves her freelance lifestyle as it allows her to move around and travel as much as she wants for both work and pleasure. She is passionate about health and wellbeing practices (meditation, counselling, self-improvement and yoga activities), so she leads a semi-active lifestyle (it ebbs and flows with active and restful). She is tech-savvy and likes to have tools that make life and her computer job more comfortable, streamlined, easy and fun.

BRAND LOYALTY

If she receives good customer service, a product is simple, easy, straightforward and transparent to use and it helps make her work-life better without breaking the bank, she's loyal.

40 Creating detailed personas helps you to develop an informed picture of the users of your product.

Claudia

54 years old social worker

Sight impaired (partially sighted)

Uses a screen magnifier and changes colours to increase contrast

Chromebook help

If you're lost, go back to the top left to re-orientate yourself.

Ashleigh

24 years old arts graduate and administrative assistant

Severely sight impaired (blind)

Uses a screen reader

Chromebook help

Screen reader quick guide:
Use Tab to move from links and form elements to the next, Shift + Tab to go back, Search + Arrow Right/Left to read text in between those.

Ron

82 years old, retired

Multiple conditions: arthritis, losing his hearing, cataracts, hip replacements

Doesn't use any assistive technology

Chromebook help

As Ron is not very technical, don't use anything which might help. For example, don't zoom into the page and don't use the keyboard to navigate.

41 Personas can be used to test particular aspects of your product, such as the accessibility of your interface.

online questionnaires or using online chat or email – aim to interview five people and record your findings. You could also look at the types of users you or a competitor has online by looking at social media followers. Once you have some data, you can then identify some common themes to enable you to create an initial persona. To create a persona, you need to imagine who you are creating your content for – make the person real rather than using general terms to describe your audience. You can do this by giving them

- A name and photo
- A job
- A status
- A location
- Characteristics
- Wants and needs
- Motivations
- Goals
- Frustrations/pain points.

This helps you think about specific uses of your product rather than talking about it in abstract terms (fig. 41).

To further expand your persona, create a list of digital touchpoints and an empathy map (see 'Empathy maps', p. 93). Identifying digital touchpoints helps you to think about a typical day or week in the life of your persona. This will help you see the different activities and interactions that take place throughout your persona's life, which can in turn help you understand how best to engage with your user.

Storytelling

Storytelling has always been a fundamental part of human society – from the earliest art and sculpture to gaming and films – and how we tell a story can be vital in helping everyone understand your product. Storytelling helps you and a design team to understand and empathize with an audience and their user journey (see 'Writing a brief', p. 34), and then to engage the user by creating a narrative and making sure that relevant content is available when a user needs it.

User stories (often used in agile and scrum processes; see 'The agile mindset', p. 22, and 'The scrum process', p. 25) describe different features of a product from the perspective of a user, helping the user to understand how a product works and how it can help them. These should be driven by the objectives for the product you are creating, be that a website, an augmented interaction or another creation. Selecting a range of user stories that are important to your product – these could be considered high-priority stories – will help you understand the different routes that can be taken through a product. There are potentially endless possible stories that can be used to map a user journey: therefore, when creating stories for your product, it is important to be able to distinguish between high- and low-priority stories – that is, what is most important to your brand and the audience.

There are six key elements of a story:

1. Characters: people (or animals or objects) who are part of your story

2. Setting: when and where your story takes place

3. Plot: the sequence of events in your story

4. Theme: the underlying ideology and central idea of the story

5. Conflict: the reason that change takes place in your story

6. Resolution: the outcome of the story.

User stories in the agile process can be further developed using the principles of INVEST (see below).

I	**Independent:** the story should be separate from other stories, so that stories can be worked on in any order
N	**Negotiable:** the story should not be something that is set in stone but a discussion point to be refined
V	**Valuable:** the story must be useful for both the user and the creators
E	**Estimable:** the size of the story, and how long it might take to create the solution, must be able to be estimated so the story can be correctly prioritized
S	**Small:** the story should be small enough that it can be completed during the time allotted for its development; if it is an epic, split it into different smaller stories
T	**Testable:** the story must be able to be tested in order to be considered complete

By bringing all these elements together, we can begin to construct user stories to help us understand the user journey. User stories follow a basic template:

As a [type of user], **I want to** [use function] **so that I can** [achieve goal].

For example:

As a person planning a holiday, **I want to** search for holiday cottages available within a specific date range **so that I can** only see the options that are relevant to me.

This is then developed into a longer, more detailed narrative called a *user scenario*, which describes the whole of a user's journey through a product – each interaction that takes place between a user's first contact with a product through to achieving their goals. User scenarios can be useful at different stages of the design process: they can be used initially to explore the potential of a project, but they can also be used to understand existing user journeys through a product – this is often informed by data that is then translated into a story to help explain an existing journey. They can also help creatives identify possible areas where the product can be improved. See page 90 for a user scenario based on the above user story.

The example on page 90 is a user scenario, but in user story terms it is known as an *epic story*. In order to help develop and refine ideas in an agile environment or for a design sprint, the story might benefit from being broken down into smaller pieces, such as 'Beryl wants to search for a holiday using a specific date range and location so that she can only see holidays relevant to her needs', which might help a team working on the booking search engine. The user scenario instead gives an overview of the user's whole experience, including their motivation, how they came to the product, and events that followed on from their use of the product. As UX designers, we need to understand that the experience of using a product and interacting with

User story

As a person planning a holiday, I want to search for holiday cottages available within a specific date range so that I can only see the options that are relevant to me.

User scenario

It is the new year and Beryl has decided that to celebrate her partner's birthday she would like to take them away on a short holiday. Next time she has a moment, she plans to find somewhere for them to stay.

That evening as Beryl is at home watching TV, an advertisement for HolidayCottagesforYou.co.uk comes on. This jogs her memory, and she grabs her smartphone and begins to search for the website. Once she arrives at the website, she immediately sees some search options to narrow down the selection of holiday cottages. She quickly filters her results and begins to look at different cottages. She doesn't find what she is looking for and goes back to adjust her search. This time she finds the perfect cottage and promptly books. She receives an email confirmation of her payment and booking, but the exact location of the cottage is still not confirmed – she only knows roughly where it is. A few days later an email from the cottage owners arrives to confirm the location.

A few months have passed, and it is just a week to go before the short holiday.

Beryl is a bit nervous because she has not heard anything from the owners or the company she booked the cottage through, but she is looking forward to the trip.

A few days later she receives an email with detailed directions as well as a welcome email reminding her of what is at the cottage so that she can make sure to pack what she needs. She feels much more at ease.

It is the day of the journey, and Beryl is excited to surprise her partner. She has received an email from the owners with last-minute reminders and instructions on what to do when they arrive. They jump in the car, Beryl enters the address the owners have given her into the satnav and they leave for the cottage. A few hours later they arrive at the cottage, and Beryl is able to follow the instructions the owner sent.

The next day the owners come to meet Beryl and her partner face to face to make sure they are happy with the accommodation and see if there is anything else they need.

Beryl and her partner have a great time at the cottage. A few days after arriving home, Beryl receives an email asking her to give feedback about the stay. Beryl says she and her partner had a great time away and plan to use the website again for future holidays.

the company behind the product does not begin and end with only the product. Considering the beginning and end of a journey outside of the product helps to clarify the types of interactions that the user and company need to make. Through this, we can help identify not only positive experiences but also the pinch points along the way. Knowledge of both can improve the quality of user experience.

Journey maps

A journey map is a visualization of the entire user experience, documenting everything a user, thinks, feels, does or encounters during their contact with a product (fig. 42). Understanding why and how your audience are going to use, or are using, your product helps you map your project objectives to your audience. The mapping of why and how users engage with your platform needs to be underpinned by good-quality personas, informed by research and data, rather than imagined ones that could easily be wrong. You will most likely find that you create a series of journey maps based on your users.

42 A partial journey map representing the beginning stages of the user scenario on page 90.

Beryl's user journey

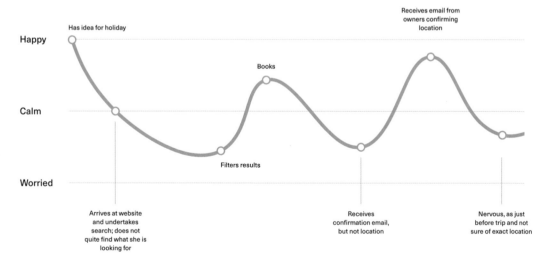

Create a journey map by:

1. Using a predefined persona. Your personas will likely influence your journey map, and you may find that you have different journeys based on your different personas. Your map might focus on a small part of the user's journey, or it could cover the whole of the journey including before and after the user interacts with the product.

2. Creating a scenario for your user with some clear expectations. Once you have a journey, you can define your scenario. This should be linked to your persona's goals – what they want to achieve – and should list the key stages of the scenario.

3. Laying out a journey with key stages identified. Now that you have a persona, a journey and a scenario, you need to consider what it is that your persona is aiming to achieve and important goals along the way. Include why, where, steps required and potential challenges.

4. Identifying any opportunities. During your user journey, what opportunities are there to improve the experience? How can any changes can be measured?

5. Storyboarding your journey. You could have a pictorial storyboard and include your character, or you could map the journey as a diagram. Make sure to show each step of the key stages of the scenario you previously identified.

Personas and journey maps form the foundation of user testing (see 'User testing', p. 94).

Empathy maps

An empathy map can help you and your team to gain a better understanding of what your users are thinking, feeling, saying, doing and hearing (fig. 43). This is useful when you are developing personas. Empathy mapping is carried out after initial user research and before a product specification is created. They can lead to useful team discussions early in the development process.

There are different types of empathy maps: a broad empathy map explores users' overall desires to use your product, while a contextual empathy map is useful for analyzing and understanding specific user issues: for example, 'Why are lots of users struggling to share content with their friends?'

43 An empathy map.

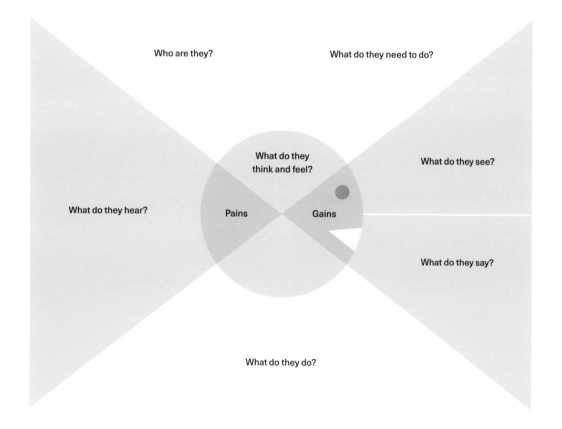

Who are they?

What do they need to do?

What do they think and feel?

What do they see?

What do they hear?

Pains

Gains

What do they say?

What do they do?

2.5 User testing

User testing puts your product in front of real-world users at different stages of the design process, giving you important data to fine-tune your product. After collecting and analyzing data, constructing personas and investigating journey maps, you may feel that you understand who your user is and how they are going to use your product, but until you put your creation in front of someone and ask them to interact with it there is no way of knowing if they will use it in the way that you expect.

This is where user testing is vital: it helps you to identify what is working and what needs improving. Each of the different design processes we looked at in part 1 included stages for testing throughout a project. Testing ideas and presenting them to audiences, be that your client or user, is essential in creating a successful outcome for your project.

In user testing, a user is asked to perform a task and talk through their thought process while someone observes their actions (fig. 44). This observation may be quite informal or it may involve different devices to measure a user's responses as they experience a product. User testing needs to be directed and supported. You cannot simply ask a user to use your product, you need to give them a task to achieve through using your product (e.g., finding a specific piece of information or booking a holiday).

User testing is not about reinventing the wheel – it is often about identifying friction within a system and making small improvements.

Even these little refinements can have a dramatic impact on the success of a product. User testing should be used at different stages of your design and development process to determine whether your product enables your users to achieve their goals with the desired ease. Just because one person in your user testing session did something unexpected does not mean that everyone will, but if you found that six out of eight of your users did the same thing, then there is a good chance most other people will as well.

You may wish to make sure that the structure of a website or page navigation is clear, or that the content is accessible and visually communicating what the product is. Or perhaps you want to test out specific user tasks or expected journeys to make sure that these are achievable without cognitively overloading the user. You might also undertake user testing after your product has gone live to better understand why macro or micro user goals are not necessarily being achieved. A/B testing and beta testing are two methods that are particularly useful for refining your product.

44 Paper prototypes can help you test out a specific user task.

A/B testing

A/B testing is a cheap and easy way to test out a new design element or feature on your website and see if it gives improved results. The process works by setting up a system that displays either your existing page (A), or your new and improved page (B) to your users. Usually, half your users see page A and half see page B. Analyzing the data from these page views can help you to decide if you should implement your new page B changes or not (fig. 45).

A/B testing is often about subtle design changes, such as new headlines, calls to action or images, rather than radical redesigns. This works alongside a quantitative approach to analyzing and developing your digital designs. It is important to make sure that you have clear goals and objectives before beginning A/B testing, otherwise you may get inconclusive results. Always be clear about the purpose of the page that you are testing and what goals you would like your users to achieve. In websites and games in particular, you need to make sure that you can measure the outcomes: for example, the amount of time

45 A/B testing. In this testing scenario, the B version has resulted in a higher conversion rate than the A version.

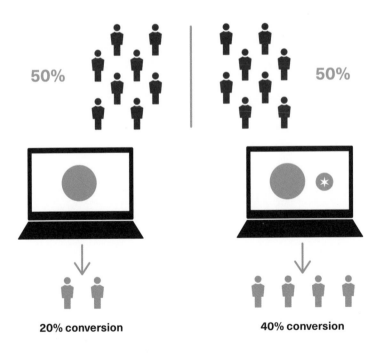

50%   50%

20% conversion   **40% conversion**

spent on a page, or the number of clicks. This should form the basis of an A/B test. A/B testing will not produce results if there are greater issues at play, such as not understanding the user's reasons for being on a website or that your product offer is not of interest to the users.

Beta testing

Beta testing is undertaken by end users to help iron out any bugs or issues prior to a product launch. Sometimes this takes place in a controlled environment where a selected group is asked to test out a new product; it can also happen in an open environment where anyone can access the test product, and might also incorporate an element of A/B testing. Beta testing is a valuable source of data, as users are encouraged to give feedback on their experiences or any issues that they may have found.

Tips for successful testing sessions

Running testing sessions in person and virtually both work, but each approach has its challenges. In-person sessions may mean that the user is in unfamiliar surroundings and also has to travel to the testing location, while in virtual sessions you have to rely on the user's device and connection working in a way that enables you to document the testing process.

During the task you need to collect as much information as possible that you can review back later. User testing does not always require a high-tech lab and expensive tools. Often you can get the data you need with just a screen recorder and a video recorder.

Whatever stage your project is at, there are some simple guidelines that can help you get the most out of your user testing:

Identify your goals and scenarios before the session. What is it that you want to achieve from the user testing? Once you are clear on this, you can start to think about the scenarios that you may wish to give to your users.

Test one person at a time, but aim to test more than one person.
It is best to test one person at a time. If you try to undertake user testing with four or five people at a time, you may find that the participants influence each other, preventing you from collecting high-quality, information-rich data. That said, you should be testing about five people in order to give you enough data and to find patterns within your dataset.

Put your user at ease. When you start your session, you may find that the user is tense and unsure of what to expect. Calmly explaining the purpose of the session and how it will work will help with this.

Get your users to talk. It is important to gather as much information as possible, and one way to do this is to get your users to 'think out loud' and constantly verbalize their thoughts to help you understand what is going on and why they are making particular choices or taking certain actions (e.g., why they are choosing to navigate or move around your product in a particular way). Another way to encourage your users to talk is through asking questions. When you do, ask open questions (rather than closed or leading questions, which can be answered yes or no) to encourage users to think further about the activity and express their thoughts, opinions and ideas, which will give you a richer set of data.

Observe – don't talk too much. It is important that you do not influence users too much during the activity that you have given them to complete, otherwise you will get false results. Of course, that does not mean that you should remain silent the whole time, and you might find that you need to prompt your users and ask them to explain why they did something or what their thinking was.

Once you have finished your user testing, you need to collate and analyze the data, identify any patterns that emerge, and then create a report or set of action points to present to your team (see 'Data collection', 'Data analysis' and 'Presenting data visually', pp. 58–75). This will inform how the project will develop moving forwards.

Part 2

Summary

In this section we have looked at the different approaches to knowing your audience. If you know your audience, you will be able to make confident, informed design decisions to improve the products you are working on and to enhance the user experience.

There are different approaches and tools to use based on which specific stage of product development you are in, from user testing to data analysis, but also on what you wish to find out. It is important to know what approaches to use, when to use them and – most importantly – the right questions to ask. Once you have this information, being able to interpret the findings and convert them into actions that help everyone is a powerful tool.

User testing

Subhrajit Das works as a lead UX designer in a team for Cloudera, a data cloud management company. They create products that data scientists or engineers in an organization can use to help them collect, collate and analyze information that helps inform the direction of the organization. Cloudera's speciality is delivering a mixture of on-premises and cloud-based solutions. Part of Subhrajit's role is to create a consistent experience across the different platforms.

Approach

One of the projects that Subhrajit is working on is an ETL (Extract, Transform, Load) pipeline. This tool helps data engineers make data usable for someone who is trying to get value out of the data. For example, Subhrajit says, 'this could involve getting data from a point of sale in Walmart or Tesco to help understand what inventory is running low in a particular store. To do this the engineers move data from the source into some sort of repository data warehouse. They then transform the data because it might not be in a format that is conducive

to analytics – there could be data missing or corrupted. The data engineer transforms the data into a different format so that someone like a business analyst can get value out of it.' As part of the development of the product, Subhrajit and the UX team at Cloudera undertook user testing in order to understand whether the product met the user's requirements and expectations and to discover and measure pain points.

Cloudera approach the development of new and existing products by forming a 'triad' of key parties: the UX team, their engineering counterparts and a product manager. The triad identifies new products or key sets of features that they wish to add to existing products. The new products or features are informed through ongoing user testing throughout the development cycle. User research determines whether the product or feature that is being built is going to solve an existing problem.

Subhrajit says, 'I know that if I understand the problem, I have already done 50 percent of my job. If you understand the right problem, you know the solution will work most of the time. If we don't identify the right problem or solution even after we deliver an update, it is not going to solve the customer's problem and it's not going to overcome the issues.' With this in mind, Subhrajit begins by setting up some customer interviews, often starting with someone who is internal to Cloudera. He says, 'I can initially use the internal person, such as a sales person, a customer support person or a subject matter expert, who is constantly in touch with customers and their issues, as a proxy for customers. This helps us bounce off some ideas and we'll get some feedback on questions that will help us identify our next steps. We will then set up some actual customers and user testing.' Subhrajit and the UX team prepare a series of unstructured open-ended questions to find out how users currently work.

If Subhrajit is developing a new product, he does some qualitative research, because he wants 'to understand what frustrates users most about their current process and how users are achieving the task right now without the help of our product. I'll have four or five questions in my mind and I will also gather questions from other stakeholders as well, such as the product manager and engineering manager.'

During the initial user research, Subhrajit and his team specifically want to gain an understanding of where the different pain points are and how users are generally using the existing product. The team will often do around five interviews, deliberately asking open and not leading questions to gain some insight. The team then analyzes the interview responses to find recurring patterns, which they use to generate a list of priorities to be tackled through the creation of different models, workflows and diagrams.

Subhrajit explains that 'during the interview/user testing process there will be two people – one to take notes and the other to ask the questions'. It is important to put the participants at ease, Subhrajit says: 'If you have already built a relationship with the user, they're much more comfortable in giving you feedback. Initially, if they are answering open-ended questions for the first time, it can be hard for them to wrap their head around why these questions are being asked. When this happens, I explain that I'm trying to understand what their current workflow is and what their pain points are right now without constraining them with what I have in mind.' For this

'If you understand the right problem, you know the solution will work most of the time.'

reason, Subhrajit says, 'it's important that we do not influence the user in any way and frame our questions in a way that is fairly open ended. But we also need to make sure that we build empathy as well.' He also says that often participants might 'not be forthcoming with their feedback because they are worried it might make Cloudera look bad or make them look bad because they're not able to do something right. So we tell them that the best help the participants can give us is honest feedback and not to worry if it's critical.

'If I just broadly asked them questions like "What are the top three frustrating experiences in your current workflow?" they might not give me three, but they will definitely give me one, like "I definitely need to do this, but I spend 20 percent of my time doing something else." And as a designer this is really useful information.' More organic conversations give the opportunity to get to the root of problems that might have been previously overlooked.

Following the qualitative research, the project team will meet to agree the key issues and then start to categorize them to find patterns. This helps them identify the pain points and gaps in users' workflow. Stakeholders then analyze and prioritize the feedback using affinity mapping (see 'Affinity mapping', p. 67). After this, the team votes on the three categories that

they think are most in need of development, and each member sketches out and shares a landing page. From this point, different workflows are created to start to resolve the issues identified. The team creates product mock-ups, which can be further refined using Cloudera's design system.

The next stage is to develop user scenarios: 'Imagine you are X and you want to do Y. How do you go about doing that?' These are agreed upon by the different stakeholders in the project. Testing user scenarios helps to validate the design assumptions and workflows. Users walk through the design mock-ups to complete these scenarios on their own, while UX designers observe whether the users are able to complete the tasks as expected or whether they are faltering somewhere. The testing team will have a pre-agreed script so they are consistent with their testing. Throughout the user testing, the participant is encouraged to give feedback and to think out loud; this helps the team understand what the participants did and did not understand, as well as details such as why they could not find a particular tool. During the testing, the note taker will use sticky notes to collect details of the test.

This cycle of development and user testing continues up to the product launch. Any issues identified close to launch are likely to be explored in the next cycle of development – this is why each new development cycle contains a mixture of updates and new features.

Thoughts on the future

Subhrajit says that automation is likely to be increasingly valuable in user testing: for example, being able to place potential designs in a space where users can test them without such high levels of observation. 'It is important to remember the purpose of user testing is to validate what you are delivering to the customer', Subhrajit says, and automation can go some way to doing this. While there will still be a need for qualitative user testing, Subhrajit believes that quantitative testing is likely to play a greater role. It is also likely to be helpful in finding specific users for testing.

Finding specialized participants who are willing to spend their time undertaking user testing can be very hard, and this is one of Subhrajit's own pain points that he would like to improve.

Subhrajit sees UX designers having a greater role to play in enterprise business as a whole. He says that 'great design is a chief value creator', and by being more 'design mature' businesses can take a more user-centric approach in every aspect of their companies. Having more designers in senior roles gives the opportunity for high-level decisions to be made that are more customer focused. This could improve user-friendly approaches to product creation, and also foster a user-focused co-design approach in human resources and sales departments.

'If you have already built a relationship with the user, they're much more comfortable in giving you feedback.'

refining your product

3.1 Designing a digital interface

In Part 1, as part of our examination of different approaches to digital design, we covered Gillian Crampton Smith's definition of good interaction design (see 'Digital design methods', p. 20), and in Part 2 we looked at different ways to build an understanding of your audience. In Part 3 we will build on this further by looking at different types of interfaces to better understand how to utilize screen-based digital media, how to structure your content, and how to visualize your product, with a view to refining your digital solutions and creating the best possible user experience on any device.

The interface is a blend of words, images and perhaps sounds through which users interact with your digital product, so these elements need to work together as effectively as possible. The interface can be thought of as both the point of interaction and the device through which the user is making the interaction. The digital medium has both virtues and drawbacks, and it is important to understand and appreciate them so that you can harness them to create an engaging user experience.

Marshall McLuhan, in his book *The Medium Is the Massage*, introduces the idea that 'all media are extensions of some human faculty . . . The wheel is an extension of the foot. The book is an extension of the eye . . . clothing an extension of the skin, electric circuitry, an extension of the central nervous system.' All of this, McLuhan says, alters the way that we see the world around us and how we interact

Network Effect (2015)

Network Effect, an interactive collage by Jonathan Harris and Greg Hochmuth, uses data visualization to investigate how we experience life online, and the effects this has on us. Users can access the project for a limited number of minutes per day, based on life expectancy where they live.

'*Network Effect* explores the psychological effects of Internet use on humanity, presenting an overwhelming assault of audiovisual material collected online.'

Jonathan Harris

Screenshot from *Network Effect*.

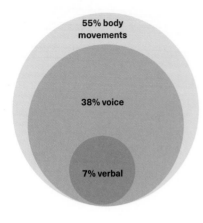

55% body movements

38% voice

7% verbal

46 Words account for only 7 percent of human communication.

with it. McLuhan says, 'In the name of "progress" our official culture is striving to force the new media to do the work of the old.' Cultivating an awareness of how we, as a society, see the media we use and how we use emerging media culturally will help you to better utilize the digital medium to create innovative solutions.

While the digital revolution has created greater opportunity for human communication, digital products still rely on forms of communication that can limit our understanding of a creator's intended message. Douglas Rushkoff, in his book *Program or Be Programmed*, discusses the work of Mele Koneya and Alton Barbour, who say only 7 percent of human communication occurs on the verbal level; 55 percent of our communication is done through body movements and 38 percent through the pitch, volume and tone of our voices (fig. 46). The challenge that this creates is that most forms of online communi-cation rely on words – the verbal level that accounts for only 7 percent of the way we communicate – and are not able to use the full range of our natural human communication skills. Because of this, the visual aspects of a digital interface are especially important.

Elements and principles of visual design

In addition to words, we are also able to engage with a user through one-way imagery and sound (with some limited haptic feedback as well). Visual elements and their display are an important part of the user experience. The principles of visual design guide designers on how best to present information. Even if you are not yourself a graphic designer, being aware of these principles will help you to create interfaces and visually structure information in a way that is effective and considered.

Elements of design

Line: connects two objects, but also directs the eye or divides objects.

Line

Colour: adds personality and emotion, and can also indicate hierarchy.

Colour

Shape and form: can be organic, geometric or abstract; they give structure or grab attention, and can connect or divide.

Shape and form

Texture: refers to the appearance of the surfaces of the objects you are creating and the feeling this evokes.

Texture

Size: affects the relationship between objects, communicating their relative importance and helping to grab attention.

Size

Value: refers to how dark or light an object's colour is; the value is relative to the background of the object: for example, on a white background a high value would be 100 percent black.

Value

Space: the empty area around an object or the space that an object takes up; helps to draw attention to important parts of the design and can improve readability (see 'Attention span and readability', p. 132).

Space

Principles of design

Contrast: Creating contrast between the different elements of your design makes it easier to distinguish between them and also to communicate a hierarchy in your content.

Alignment: Aligning objects in your design helps to create connections and cohesiveness on a page or screen. Grids and columns help you to lay out your content.

Repetition: Recurring elements bring consistency and a sense of place in a design, and also help to create pattern and order.

Proximity: The way you group visual objects together creates a sense of belonging among them and helps with the organization of elements on a page or screen.

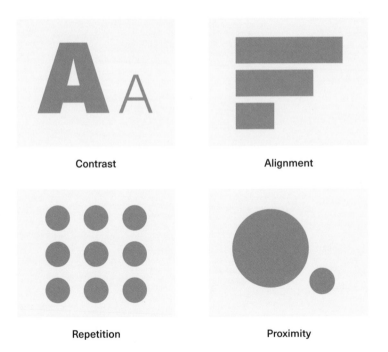

Contrast

Alignment

Repetition

Proximity

Gestalt principles

Gestalt is a German word meaning 'shape' or 'form'. Gestalt principles explain how the eye perceives visual objects, expanding on the classic design principles in detail that is relevant to visual designers. They were proposed by three German psychologists, Max Wertheimer, Kurt Koffka and Wolfgang Köhler, who focused on understanding how people see the world around them. Gestalt principles are important in UX design because they help us design interfaces that users can take in at a glance – vital when users typically spend only seconds on a webpage (see 'Attention span and readability', p. 132).

Similarity

Similarity: We naturally want to find objects that are similar among a mass of others.

Continuation

Continuation: Our eye will most likely follow a line, even if it changes colour or shape.

Closure

Closure: We prefer closed shapes, so our minds will automatically fill in parts of an image that are not there.

Figure/ground: Related to *closure*; we look first for solid objects, and we tend to see foreground first – unless an image is ambiguous, like the popular illusion Rubin's vase, which can be perceived as either a vase or two faces, depending on what part of the negative space you concentrate on.

Figure / ground

Proximity

Proximity: When we group multiple objects together, our mind sees them as a single object.

Symmetry and order: Our mind will break down complex objects into more simple objects.

Symmetry / order

Common fate: If we see shapes or lines moving or pointing in the same direction, our mind will group them together.

Common fate

These elements and principles do not exist in isolation – there is clear crossover between the different groups of concepts. It is how you use them together that helps create a unique design. It is also important to be aware of these rules so that you can consciously break them. Some of the most effective designs stand out because of a deliberately broken principle. But it is important not to break all of the elements and principles at the same time, as this can easily result in a mess.

Skeuomorphic and flat design

There are a number of different visual approaches to creating screen-based solutions that you can take. Some of these borrow from the real world, while others are more abstract.

In the digital space, *skeuomorphic design* takes objects from the real world and recreates them virtually. While this might seem like a contradiction of the digital medium, it makes digital interfaces recognizable, reassuring and understandable, helping users interact with a new device. Skeuomorphic design is evident in many aspects of digital interfaces, from the envelope used as an icon for an email program to the green cloth background of a blackjack table in a gaming app or the rounded buttons of a calculator – these all borrow from the real world

GALLERY – PAGE 113

to help make an interface welcoming and relatable (figs 47–49).

In contrast to skeuomorphic design, *flat design* does not borrow to such an extent from the real world – rather, it embraces the digital space through the use of flat icons and colour. This creates a clearer legibility through a focus on information by removing what some might describe as an unnecessary clutter of materials and textures

GALLERY – PAGE 114

(figs 50–52).

Skeuomorphic and flat design are transitional in their translation of the real world to the virtual one, and as we all become more comfortable with interacting with the digital space there is potential that we will become further removed from its skeuomorphic origins.

Gallery 3.1: Skeuomorphic and flat design

LEFT | **47** The skeuomorphic page-turning animation in Apple's iBooks app replicates the real-world experience of reading a book.

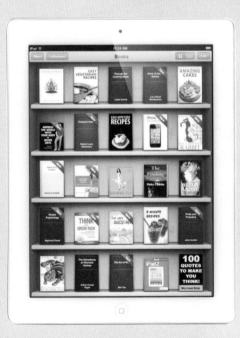

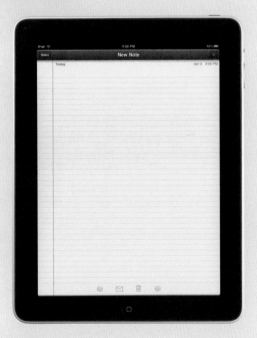

48 Early versions of Apple's app interfaces were heavily skeuomorphic, such as the bookshelf in iBooks.

49 Apple Notes for iPad used an interface design based on a physical notepad.

Gallery 3.1: Skeuomorphic and flat design

50 Apple's design practice has gradually moved away from skeuomorphism towards flat design, as shown in these iterations of the Calculator app interface.

51 Microsoft firmly embraced flat design with the tile icons in the Windows 8 interface.

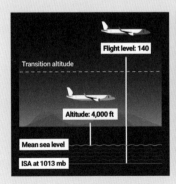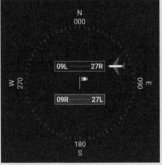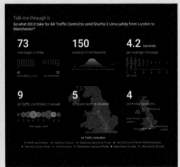

52 In *Plane Talking*, a project for the UK's National Air Traffic Services, Beyond Words Studio used flat design to explore how NATS air traffic controllers guided a flight from London to Manchester.

Cognitive friction

Alan Cooper introduced the term *cognitive friction* in his book *The Inmates Are Running the Asylum.* He describes cognitive friction as 'the resistance encountered by a human intellect when it engages with a complex system of rules that changes as the problem changes'. Objects in the virtual space can constantly change behaviours, while in the physical space an object's behaviour is more often predictable and not likely to change. For example, a virtual on/off button can change what it does depending on many variables, and therefore what is turned on or off could change each time you press it; however, a physical on/off button attached to a machine will always do the same thing. Understanding cognitive friction helps you to create an experience and quality of interaction that is successful for the user.

An unexpected change of behaviour creates an interruption in the process of thought or actions, and will often leave a user confused or irritated with their experience. As a result, they may not remember what they are doing, why they are there or what they were trying to achieve. Understanding cognitive friction and where it might occur will help you design a successful user experience. Understanding the user and user testing play a key part in identifying pain points and areas where cognitive friction might occur (see 'Understanding the user', p. 84).

Cognitive friction does not always have to be a bad thing; it can be purposefully created in a design. However, it really only has a place in experimental interfaces where the interface itself is deliberately challenging the user to question the experience itself, or as a way to encourage users to become active and to solve problems themselves and learn from this. But this has to be undertaken in the right environment with users who are willing to be part of this process, such as in gamification.

Intuitive design

On the other end of the spectrum from cognitive friction is intuitive design. This is where objects and items respond in ways that a user would expect – not in an Orwellian *1984* way where everything is identical and globally controlled, but in a way that creates a consistent experience for a user. For example, if you create a design in which hyperlinks in a body of text are underlined and pink, then all links throughout the product need to be styled in the same way. This sits well with, and is part of, design systems and design and gestalt principles. Intuitive design is also concerned with how something acts when you interact with it. Not only should elements consistently look the same, they should consistently behave the same way when a user interacts with them. (Remember Gillian Crampton Smith's definition of good interaction design; see 'Digital design methods', p. 20.)

Intuitive design connects to, and generates tension between, a skeuomorphic approach and a more abstracted flat design approach. In an attempt to create an intuitive and recognizable experience, it is tempting to choose a skeuomorphic design. However, as we become more comfortable with interacting with digital interfaces, we can become distanced from our original cultural associations with the real-world objects these interfaces were originally developed from. This leads us to become more functional and abstract in our approach to solutions that are informed by the digital medium we are using and the audience we are creating them for (fig. 53).

53 Car key designs at Mercedes-Benz are becoming increasingly intuitive (right to left below). Ultimately, car keys may become completely abstract – a phone app rather than a physical device.

One design, many devices

We have already looked at how users can have different experiences even when using the same platform in a multiplatform space (see 'Same platforms, different experience', p. 46). An extension of this is understanding the varying demands a user might have depending on the device they are using.

There are some practical considerations to designing for different devices and different screen sizes, beginning with the challenge of screen real estate and the value of *above the fold* (visible before scrolling) and *below the fold* (not visible unless scrolling) content. It is vital that you understand your audience and how they are going to use your product on different devices before you begin designing your digital interface.

When you create a screen-based design, it is important to consider the different devices that it will be viewed on, as each have different shapes and sizes. Generally, you will need to design for mobile phone, tablet and desktop screen sizes. It is currently considered good practice to first design for the smallest screen, usually a mobile phone, and then scale up to a desktop computer, because most interactions happen on a mobile or other small-screen device (fig. 54). In general, you are going to have more design challenges when creating solutions for a smaller screen. The benefit of starting with the smaller screen is that you will overcome a lot of the challenges early on in the design process, rather than having to resolve them at a later stage in the process, which can often be more difficult.

GALLERY – PAGE 122

Designing for mobile first also enables you to consider the different design elements that are required and which are most important for your users, while also taking into account that users most often navigate using their fingers rather than a mouse (fig. 55). When designing for a mobile screen it is important to consider the following:

Size and proportions of an image. How an image is displayed can vary greatly. A mobile screen is likely to have a different aspect ratio than a desktop screen – a desktop screen is often wider, while a phone screen is often taller.

Columns and grids. Using a grid enables you to quickly lay out the different elements in your design and align these to create a consistent design and experience. This can help you guide the reader quickly to the most important content. The width of a desktop means that you have the option to include many columns of content on your screen, but if you replicate this on a mobile phone the content can become too small to be legible. Having two columns often works for images, but most of the time only one column is needed, especially if there is a large amount of text to also include.

Typography. Consider how the typography is going to be displayed on a smaller screen. What size will it need to be so that it is legible, and how will this change on different screens?

Page hierarchy. Plan your above-the-fold and below-the-fold content carefully. With smaller screens, the order in which you display your content becomes even more important. It is good practice to indicate when there is more content below.

54 Mobile-first design.

Navigation. On a small screen it is much more difficult to show your site navigation and your content at the same time. For this reason, the hamburger menu icon (consisting of three horizontal lines and often visible at the top of a website) has become popular in small-screen layouts. This enables the menu to be accessible as a layer over the content; it does not need to be constantly visible and taking up lots of space.

Once you have addressed these elements and questions, you can begin to consider how the structure and the display of content will change as the screen size increases.

Beyond the flat screen

We are concentrating primarily on designing for screen-based visual solutions, but the design methods and approaches that we have looked at are transferable to emerging non-screen-based platforms, such as voice user interfaces and virtual and augmented reality. *Voice user interfaces*, which use speech recognition, allow users to access technology through voice commands. These interfaces are becoming increasingly popular in our everyday lives, from asking our phones to make a call or message to instructing our home system to dim lights or play specific music (fig. 56). It is likely that, in the future, these interfaces will be found in many other areas of our lives, from voice-activated locks to virtual assistants that can listen to and tran-scribe your meetings and then write up notes. Ethics and privacy are key concerns as these technologies become more widespread, but as UX designers it is important to understand how to create solutions that can be accessed through voice commands.

GALLERY – PAGE 123

Designing for a voice user interface, like any other digital solution, begins with understanding your user, including mapping user jour-neys, user testing, and identifying and addressing any cognitive friction that may occur during use of your product. In addition, you should also consider the personality of your voice user interface, as this will have a large impact on how a user perceives and interacts with your creation.

Is the interface voice old or young? Does it have an accent? How is it giving feedback? Is it serious, informal or even sarcastic?

There might not be a screen in your interaction, so understanding when to use the voice user interface and what the user might ask for and how they might ask is important. For example, if the user asks an ambiguous question with many possible answers, it may be difficult to succinctly communicate using voice (think of search results on a screen); however, a simple request, such as adding a diary entry or playing a specific piece of music, has clear outcomes that can easily be delivered through a voice user interface. It is vital to know when to use the voice-activated interface and when to not use it.

Virtual reality and augmented reality are other digital solutions that go beyond a simple screen-based interface. An *augmented reality* product combines a visual interface with a real-world interaction (figs 57–58, 60, 62). Often this means that the interface is simple and reduced, as the interaction involves moving the device physically around to locate or navigate through the app.

GALLERY – PAGE 123

A *virtual reality* product gives priority to the environment itself rather than an external interface (figs 59, 61). The user experience is likely to be more integrated into the visual environment, so the narrative and user flow of the experience is likely to need careful consideration. Different cues can help users navigate through a virtual space: for example, a sound could attract the user to an area or object, or a visual cue such as a shadow or bright light could warn of danger.

GALLERY – PAGE 124

A virtual reality product could be modelled on an existing real-world space, such as a gallery or museum, and enable users to experience spaces that are too far away to travel to, or they could be imagined realities. Virtual reality is increasingly popular as a space to play games, but it also has great potential to be used in other spaces such as work environments and industrial spaces: for example, you could use a virtual space to meet face to face with a group of colleagues who are all over the world, or you could create a drawing that is life-size.

Gallery 3.1: One design, many devices

55 A mobile-first approach to interface design, such as that adopted by Airbnb, means an interface will scale easily between different devices, from phone to tablet to desktop computer.

Gallery 3.1: Beyond the flat screen

LEFT **56** Amazon's Alexa Echo Dot is a small smart speaker that enables you to play music, make phone calls, access the internet, and control connected devices using a voice user interface.

BOTTOM **57** Eloise Calandre's *Red House* is a site-specific augmented reality design using real-world markers to link virtual content to physical objects and create a game with the promise of uncovering something otherwise hidden. Players assemble a puzzle based on clues in physical space, made manifest via a phone screen. Eloise says, 'I think of augmented reality as a tool for bringing together physical and virtual in a similar way to early forms of photography – a technology which, in its infancy, appeared to audiences as a combination of magic, physics and mechanical process.'

58 The Pokémon Go app uses augmented reality to mix a virtual game with real-world locations.

59 *A Curious Game of Croquet*, a virtual reality installation by Preloaded, on display at the Victoria and Albert Museum, London, 2021.

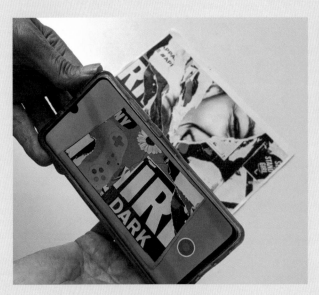

60 Chris Arran's *Flower Power* (2022) is an augmented reality artwork viewable through the Artivive app.

61 The virtual reality interface of the Google Tilt brush enables artists to draw in a digital space. Glen Keane demonstrates on *The Late Late Show with James Corden*, 2017.

62 Microsoft's HoloLens demonstrates the potential for augmented reality in real-world medical applications.

Embracing the digital medium

Fred Deakin has had a varied career that has always naturally traversed many different media: he started as a DJ; was one half of the band Lemon Jelly, selling over half a million records; and then founded and directed the digital agency Airside for 14 years.

Approach

At each stage of his journey, Fred has been interested in creating interactive experiences, from immersive club experiences in the 1980s and 90s to interactive installations. Fred has always enjoyed embracing the challenge of new technologies and the creative opportunities that come with them. Working across different mediums and ideas, Fred has always operated in a multiplatform environment. Collaborating with different creatives has been key to how he approaches different projects and utilizes each medium.

Fred describes each of his projects 'as delivering a piece of content'. He wants to give his audience 'the full package', and each of his projects incorporates a range of platforms and media to create different outputs. He sees his drive to create multiplatform solutions as an artist and practitioner stemming from being naturally creative and being able to allow ideas to creatively emerge without limiting himself to a single established medium or set of solutions. Using a range of different platforms enables Fred to produce uniquely creative solutions.

In 2012, Fred collaborated with programmer and animator Marek Bereza, music producer James Bulley and former Airside co-director Nat Hunter to create the audiovisual interactive installation *Electricity Comes from Other Planets* for France's national digital museum La Gaîté Lyrique. The installation featured eight 'planets' that generated music and animation in response to the audience's movement.

This was later followed by *Thirteen Cycles*, a Theatre and Technology Award-nominated immersive multisensory space, in which Katy Schutte and Chris Mead of Project2 improvised and acted the characters, dialogue and story and Fred created the soundtrack. *Thirteen Cycles* used motion sensors and projection mapping to create a visual environment that enabled

Fred Deakin, *Electricity Comes from Other Planets* (2012), interactive audiovisual installation.

the set to respond to the improvisations of the actors, using VR controllers attached to the actors' wrists. Fred says, 'The functionality emerged in the course of the creative process, and I think the crucial thing about that was that we were trying to make a specific show and deliver it to an audience and the show evolved at the same time as the tech did.'

Fred has applied some of this same approach in his project *The Lasters*, a science-fiction rock opera concept album. While at its heart an album, it is a multiplatform and collaborative product. The project outputs include vinyl, USB and Spotify releases; live performances; a documentary film; special edition stained-glass-window lightboxes; and special edition signed poster prints. The album cover features interactive augmented reality, with different parts of the cover playing different elements of the tracks when a tablet or mobile device is hovered over them. Fred says, 'If you had four devices pointing at each of the four images, you would have a four-part harmony.' Fred's live performances

utilize projection mapping, featuring a mixture of animation and live footage to support the narrative being constructed through the music. The animation has been repurposed so that it can be played while listening to the song on Spotify.

Thoughts on the future

When thinking about the future, Fred says that there are many great opportunities, but they can only be realized by bringing together a great range of people in collaboration, where ideas start to merge and combine with 'technology to input into the creativity and creative have an input to technology'. Fred says that,

as the future beckons, 'the digital landscape will be completely unrecognizable'. He talks about the metaverse, the next evolution of the internet where different groups of people can meet to play, learn, create, work, interact and form meaningful relationships in virtual environments. He envisions 'immersive devices beyond smart devices that will completely change our experience of what is digital'.

LEFT **Fred Deakin, *The Lasters* (2019), science-fiction concept album with augmented reality posters and album artwork.**

BELOW ***The Lasters* live performance with projection mapping.**

3.2 Structuring content

When you are designing and creating a digital product, such as a website, it is easy to get carried away with how something looks and functions, but it is equally important to consider what it is you are truly trying to communicate – the words as well as the imagery.

The organizing of content across a product so that everything is where a user expects it to be is called *information architecture* (IA); it is underpinned by the cognitive theories behind gestalt principles (see 'Gestalt principles', p. 111). IA crosses over with good UX design; if your product has good IA then it will have a positive impact on the UX of your site. For this reason, IA requires an understanding of your audience and their purpose in using your product so that you can identify the most important content and structure it effectively.

IA should help you identify what the priorities of your product are and where they should go. You do this by

- Understanding your competitors
- Defining your content
- Creating sitemaps and wireframes.

At each of the above stages, user testing, user interviews and user flow diagrams will help inform the IA of your product.

For example, by creating an initial list of key section titles and under-taking a card-sorting activity you will start to understand how your users make connections between titles; or by creating user flow diagrams and simple click-through tasks you can understand how a user might navigate a site before expensive investment in high-fidelity mock-ups or even coding. (For more on this, see 'User testing', p. 94; we'll look at user flow diagrams and mock-ups in 'Visualizing your product', p. 136.)

Validity of content

In recent years there has been a lot of media attention given to 'fake news'. For this reason, making sure that your design demonstrates to your audience that the content you are presenting is trustworthy and reliable is even more important. Part of a product's authenticity is communicated visually, but just as much is communicated through detail in the content.

When presenting content in your design (e.g., an article or blog post), giving prominence to the following elements will help reinforce the content's validity:

- **Source of information:** Make it clear where the content comes from.

- **References:** Include links to the sources that were used for the content. Consider what these sources are; ask yourself 'Are they trustworthy?' and 'Are they from a broad range of views?'

- **Date:** Make it clear when the content was created. Over time, ideas and values can change. Adding a date will give context to the information.

- **Author:** By identifying who wrote an article or blog post, you can show why the content should be read; authors who are experts in their field can add credibility to your website.

Attention span and readability

Users do not stay on webpages for very long, so it is important that you focus the content of your product so that it quickly and clearly communicates what it is. Understanding how to keep your users' attention will help you to create a successful product.

When you provide content to users, you need to make sure it is written and structured in a way that all your users can easily understand it. Content writers manage part of this process – such as ensuring appropriate lexical density and incorporating keywords that help search engines find your website – but there are other elements that fall under design, including elements such as typography, use of colour and line length.

Visually dividing text into manageable chunks can also help readers navigate information. You can do this using

- Subheadings
- Bullet points or numbered lists
- Pull quotes
- Images.

Including these structural elements helps make content clear and understandable for users, but they also help a search engine understand what is important on the page, which is necessary to drive the right sort of traffic to your website.

When you create high-fidelity mock-ups during a product visualization stage (see 'High-fidelity mock-ups', p. 144), make sure you give examples of the different page elements that you need to include: different heading levels and how they will look; page titles and how long they might be, based on keywords identified during SEO research; and typesetting to support readability at all screen sizes.

A study by Chao Liu and colleagues from Microsoft Research found that users do not stay on webpages very long, but if they don't leave the page within the first 10 seconds they will usually stay for at least two minutes. It is crucial that your product grabs the user's attention quickly.

Search engine optimization

Search engine optimization (SEO) has the goal of driving more traffic to a website by listing a site in search engine results above other sites. SEO was once considered to be the only way to drive traffic to your site, but now it is one of many, with social media platforms also playing an important role. SEO is still an important aspect of your website. Though it is something often perceived as a bit of a dark art, this is not really the case – it just requires a good understanding of who your audience is and how you want them to find you and your content.

SEO needs careful planning and also measurement, with measurement informing both the planning and the results. While there are a number of technical considerations, such as the speed of your website or page redirections, your primary concern as a UX designer is understanding the planned approach to SEO so that you can apply it in a design environment.

The earlier you can integrate SEO considerations into a design the more effective they will be. The first step is to be clear on what your business and project objectives are, know who your audience is, understand how you are going to measure success, and integrate both qualitative and quantitative measuring.

When you use a search engine, it applies a complicated algorithm to find what it believes to be the most relevant results for you by evaluating how the content of webpages is written and ranking that content in order of relevance. The search engine will respond to semantic and subject-specific themes as well as related terms. The algorithm is constantly being tweaked and refined, but the most important aspect of planning for good SEO in the long term is to make sure that your site is trusted and that your content is unique to your site (see 'Validity of content', p. 131).

Search engine optimization

Miracle Inameti-Archibong is head of SEO for Erudite, a technical marketing company, and also a speaker, trainer and mentor. Erudite is a boutique digital agency that works with national and global brands to help them to develop, embed and understand the value and importance of technical marketing. Miracle manages the SEO team, leading client strategy and maintaining an overview of the clients. She works with brand teams to support them in understanding the importance of using key design and content elements in bringing users to their websites.

Approach

Miracle describes SEO like guiding customers to a store: 'If you have a physical shop, how do people know it's there? And how do they find what's in it? Then, once a customer has found you, how do they find the department in your store? And how do they check out quickly and get that satisfaction of buying something from your store?' Miracle goes on to say,

'If you focus on your users, making sure that you are getting them to do what they want to do quickly with satisfaction, then there is no need to complicate things.'

SEO is important to consider in the product creation process, because it helps designers and developers to evaluate how easy it is for users to

- Find the site
- Understand the site
- Navigate the site
- Buy on the site
- Use the service.

By doing all this, users know you exist. Miracle says, 'You can build the most beautiful site out there, but if no one knows you exist you're just wasting your time.'

At the beginning of a project, during the onboarding process, you need to understand how to use SEO to inform your product and help you to develop your content. Miracle says that this is often accomplished through data stories. The data for these is collected from user analytics tools and heatmaps – a visual representation of where users click, move and scroll on a site – and recordings of user interactions with the website. If you are creating a new project, you can also look up competitors to understand the industry landscape. All of this will equip you to undertake user analysis and user behaviour analysis, which in turn, Miracle says, 'enables you to set out testing theories and hypotheses'.

In one key project, Erudite worked with a client to help them increase their mobile conversion rates. The project's success was aided by early integration of SEO, which meant that the client and the developers could consider and embed the different key elements into the creation from the outset rather than try to retrofit them at a later stage.

Thoughts on the future

Miracle sees the future as continuing the ever-increasing proliferation of data and sharing of information, which, she says, provides an opportunity to do so much more, especially with approaches such as behavioural analysis. She says that this should enable designers to focus on creating a much more tailored experience for users. Miracle balances this with the caveat that with all the instant gratification already available 'it is scary to think what will be next'. For example, voice user interfaces are convenient and 'convenience sells, so when you allow a device access to your data in such a way to make your life more convenient, are people aware of what they have consented to?' The tension between ethics, users' awareness of what they are sharing and the drive of the technology companies will be the thing to watch.

'You can build the most beautiful site out there, but if no one knows you exist you're just wasting your time.'

3.3 Visualizing your product

Visualizing your product involves more than just creating a set of beautiful detailed images to show how the product should look. There are a number of key stages that help you to identify and focus on specific aspects of the product, refining your design as you work through the process.

If the client asks for an image size to be changed, this creates a large amount of work in the final stages of the design process compared to simply redrawing a rectangle on a sketch in an early visualization stage. There are a number of key visualization stages in the design process to help along the way with such issues:

- User journey maps
- Sitemaps and user flow diagrams
- Wireframes
- Low-fidelity or paper prototypes
- High-fidelity mock-ups and clickable prototypes.

Each stage should be informed by the overarching design brief and an understanding of what the overall objectives are, as well as any existing design systems and brand guidelines. Each stage is designed to build upon the previous stage and inform the next, allowing you to focus on the specific task in hand rather than risk becoming over-whelmed by having to consider too many elements at the same time.

The visualization process also enables you to work in a team with the client and potential users so that at each stage there is opportunity to collect feedback and refine the design, and also to keep everyone up to date with the progress of the project and expectations.

Once you have defined your product (see 'Understanding the client', p. 32), a vital part of the design process is planning the structure and content of your product. This is undertaken through sitemaps, user flow diagrams and wireframes, which build off user journey maps developed in earlier stages of user research (see 'Journey maps', p. 91).

Sitemaps

Sitemaps show the overall structure of your product, revealing the hierarchy of information and helping you consider how users will navigate the product – this will be informed by your audience analysis and the project goals. Sitemaps are created only after user stories and user flows are established and work together with user flow diagrams to map the product. Both are needed to inform the creation of wireframes for user testing in the next stage of visualization.

Sitemaps can be created in different ways. The example here is digitally created (fig. 63), but try planning and laying it out using sticky notes first to test out different structures. When you create your sitemap, it is likely that you are not going to know all the final content for your product, so concentrate on the different sections and sub-sections and the types of material that might appear in each part. This will help you to identify templates for different aspects of your design.

For example, it is likely that your homepage will be different from any other page on your website, but if you have found that you have pages of content where the structure of the design repeats itself, such as a set of categories of articles (listicle, long-form, moving-image, etc.), these can form the basis of different key templates. Templates will save you time and help to create a consistent experience across your product: for example, you only need to create one layout for a particular category, as that layout will be used across all pages in that

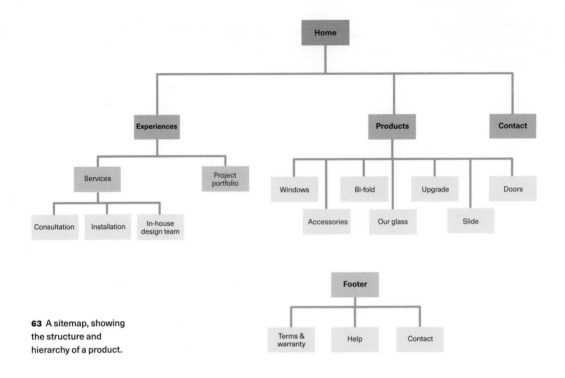

63 A sitemap, showing the structure and hierarchy of a product.

category. Make a note of any templates you identify so that you can include them in the wireframe.

User flow diagrams

A user flow diagram shows the key sections of a product, similar to a sitemap, but it does not show the details of each page; instead, it concentrates on one particular user flow through your product (fig. 64). Each stage in the user journey is laid out (indicated in fig. 64 by rectangular boxes), along with the choices or decisions that the user needs to make along the way (indicated by diamonds).

We looked at user stories and user scenarios, as well as user journeys, in 'Understanding the user' (see p. 84). In that stage of the design process, we were interested in the whole user journey, including the user's thoughts and feelings, whereas a user flow diagram is focused only on the user's interactions with your product.

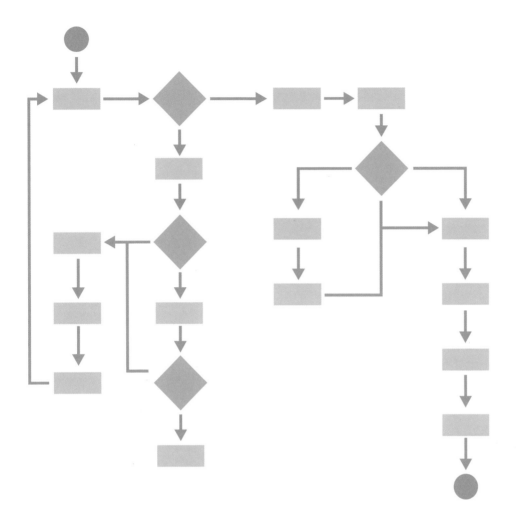

A user flow diagram is created based on personas and user journeys developed during earlier user research stages. These will help you to understand what a user is going to want to get from your product and at what point in the journey they are going to need specific information.

Any product you design is likely to have a number of different goals for your users, and these should be reflected in your user flow diagrams. For example, with an e-commerce website, your main aim – called a *macro goal* or *macro conversion* – may be to sell something, but you will also have a number of smaller goals – *micro goals* or *micro conversions* – such as informing your audience how to find

64 A user flow diagram, showing a user's journey through a product.

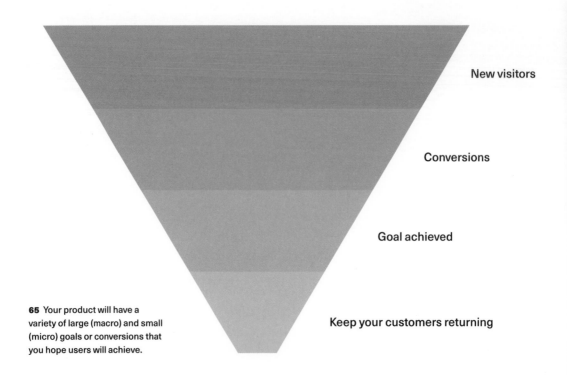

New visitors

Conversions

Goal achieved

65 Your product will have a variety of large (macro) and small (micro) goals or conversions that you hope users will achieve.

Keep your customers returning

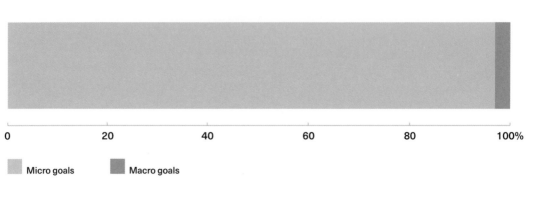

0   20   40   60   80   100%

Micro goals   Macro goals

66 Macro goals are often completed by only a tiny percentage of users. The majority of users will complete micro goals.

your nearest shop or start following you on a social media channel (these are similar to the high- and low-priority stories mentioned in 'Storytelling', see p. 87).

Understanding these different goals will help you map them to your personas and user flow diagrams, ensuring that they are reflected in your product's content and structure. Macro goals are often achieved by only a very small number of people who visit your site: for an e-commerce site, this can be about 2–4 percent of the site's visitors, so catering for the other 96–98 percent of your audience as well is very important (figs 65–66).

Wireframes

A wireframe, sometimes referred to as a low-fidelity (lo-fi) mock-up, works in a similar way to a sitemap but at an individual section level, such as a page on a website. The wireframe works to illustrate the structure, hierarchy and navigation of a page without being distracted by colour, images and typography. Wireframes use a grid and column structure that contains blocks where content would be; they might include some example headings, menu titles, placeholder text and grey blocks to represent images, but nothing more.

The examples here have been digitally drawn (fig. 67), but often a wireframe will start life as a hand-drawn sketch that can then be developed into a digital version or used as the basis for low-fidelity or paper prototypes. The purpose of a wireframe is to quickly communicate the overall structure of a product as a visual representation. The proposed structure and navigation can then be tested, but the wireframe enables you to easily make changes to the overall design before too much of the detailed design work has been undertaken.

The wireframes you initially create will be based on the different sections and types of content that you identified in your sitemap. Once you have created your initial set of wireframes and collected feedback from stakeholders, it is likely that you will then need to create a more complete set of wireframes in order to undertake some user testing using clickable wireframes and specific user tasks.

The wireframes you produce should be for the screen size you are designing for (fig. 67). This means that you need to produce three variations of the same design (mobile phone, tablet and desktop) to show how the design will look on each of the screens.

67 Wireframes represent the structure of individual sections of a website, rather than showing the whole product like a sitemap does.

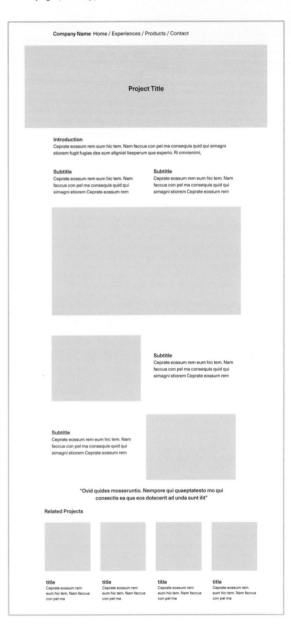

Portfolio page (desktop)

Company Name Home / Experiences / Products / Contact

Introduction
Ceprate eossum rem eum hic tem. Nam faccus con pel ma consequis quid qui simagni stiorem fugit fugias des eum aligniat liaeperum que experio.

Portfolio

Title
Ceprate eossum rem eum hic tem.
Nam faccus con pel ma consequis quid

Title
Ceprate eossum rem eum hic tem.
Nam faccus con pel ma consequis quid

Click here

Services

Title
Ceprate eossum rem eum hic tem. Nam faccus con pel ma consequis quid

Title
Ceprate eossum rem eum hic tem. Nam faccus con pel ma consequis quid

Title
Ceprate eossum rem eum hic tem. Nam faccus con pel ma consequis quid

Title
Ceprate eossum rem eum hic tem. Nam faccus con pel ma consequis quid

Click here

Product Highlights

Title
Ceprate eossum rem eum hic tem. Nam faccus con pel ma consequis quid

Title
Ceprate eossum rem eum hic tem. Nam faccus con pel ma consequis quid

Title
Ceprate eossum rem eum hic tem. Nam faccus con pel ma consequis quid

Title
Ceprate eossum rem eum hic tem. Nam faccus con pel ma consequis quid

Portfolio page (mobile)

Company Name

Introduction
Ceprate eossum rem eum hic tem.
Nam faccus con pel ma consequis quid
qui simagni stiorem fugit fugias des

Title
Ceprate eossum rem eum hic tem.
Nam faccus con pel ma consequis quid
qui simagni stiorem fugit fugias des

View more examples

Title
Ceprate eossum rem eum hic tem.
Nam faccus con pel ma consequis quid
qui simagni stiorem fugit fugias des

View more examples

68 Paper prototypes can help you plan the navigation of your product.

69 Low-fidelity prototyping is also useful for planning the structure of your product.

Low-fidelity prototypes

Low-fidelity prototypes – also called paper prototypes – are a way to quickly and easily test out ideas and user journeys. A paper prototype should focus on navigation, user journeys and features that you want to test out. It enables you to test how a product will work without distracting users with the final design elements.

A paper prototype is often very basic and hand drawn, made with materials such as paper, sticky notes, pens, pencils and scissors (fig. 68). The prototype should be a series of sketches that show the layout of your product, which you can test with users or your team (fig. 69). The testing process involves you acting as the computer: when the user taps on an option on your sketch (simulating a click), you respond by putting in front of them the piece of paper that represents the corresponding page. You can watch the user navigate your product and see if your ideas about how the product is going to work are right or if they need refining.

High-fidelity mock-ups

GALLERY – PAGE 150

Once you have defined your objectives and completed user testing, sitemaps and user flow diagrams, a clearer picture of your product will have emerged and you will be ready to create a set of high-quality or high-fidelity (hi-fi) mock-ups (figs 71–72). It is often tempting to create hi-fi visuals early on, but they will not be as thoroughly informed as if you wait for this later stage. This is not to say that the hi-fi visual design of your product should be given any less importance. The 'aesthetic usability effect', as it is known, means that often users will perceive a pleasing design as being more usable and will be more willing to overlook minor usability issues, but because of this it is important to undertake usability testing before and during the final hi-fi visualization stage. As part of user testing at the hi-fi stage, interactive click-through examples are produced for users to try out.

Hi-fi visuals bring together all of the elements for your design; they communicate not only the structure, navigation and user experience of your creation, but also details such as colours, fonts, imagery and more.

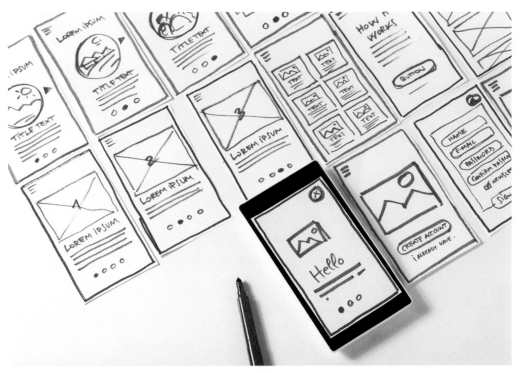

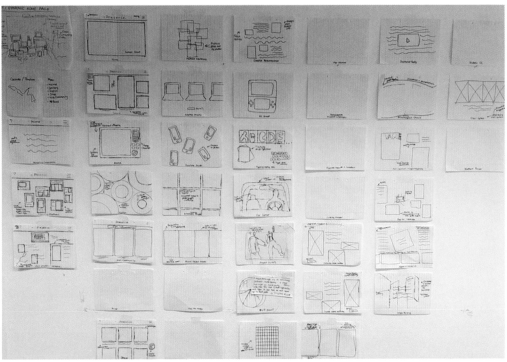

A hi-fi visualization needs to demonstrate the following:

Visual consistency. Think back to the rules of good interaction design (see 'Digital design methods', p. 20). If a user clicks from one page to another, they need to know that they are still on the same website.

Branding. It is important to make sure that the product has strong, identifiable branding that is consistent with any other platforms that the brand operates on.

Clarity. The design of the content should give a clear sense of what can be done without overwhelming the user.

Typography and type size. The size of text is often much larger on screens than it is in print. We hold different devices at different distances from our eyes, and for this reason, designers need to ensure that users can clearly read all text on all devices, while still maintaining a clear hierarchy of information.

Language style. What is the style and approach of the language that is being used in the content, and how does this fit with the goals of the project? Even though at this stage your hi-fi mock-ups are likely to still contain placeholder text, any titles and navigation elements should reflect the intended goals.

Image size and type. The design needs to take account of the style and size of the content compared to different elements. This is specifically relevant when designing for different devices and screen sizes.

Validity of content and authenticity. While wireframes should include elements that contribute towards creating valid content, the hi-fi mock-up should bring these elements together and also seek to reinforce the validity through the presentation of the content.

Thumb zone and finger-friendly design. Mock-ups for handheld devices should consider where the content is on the screen, how easy it is to reach and the size of the element that requires an interaction (fig. 70).

Motion or movement. If there is any form of animation of elements or movement, you should seek to communicate this in your hi-fi mock-up.

Design principles. Make sure that you are appropriately applying the principles of visual design throughout your product and the grid that your design is built on (see 'Principles of design', p. 110).

70 When designing for large-screen smartphones, it is important to consider where your content will fall on the screen and what your user will be able to easily reach with their thumbs.

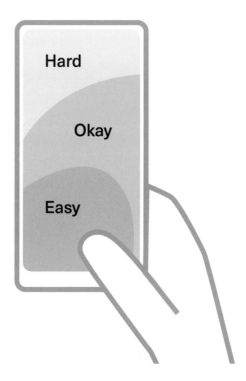

Accessibility

In every element of your product, you also need to take accessibility into account. According to UK guidelines, accessibility means 'making your content and design clear and simple enough so that most people can use it without needing to adapt it, while supporting those who do need to adapt things'. The World Wide Web Consortium (W3C) and the Americans with Disabilities Act provide further guidelines and best practices for accessibility, including in digital spaces. In your hi-fi mock-ups, you should aim to

- Make sure that text colours are clearly visible against your background
- Make sure content is structured logically and can be navigated and read by a screen reader
- Not to use colour as the only way to explain or distinguish something
- Use meaningful headings and labels, making sure that any accessible labels match or closely resemble the label you're using in the interface
- Use headings and spacing to group related content
- Make sure features look consistent and behave in predictable ways and consider how this will work across different device/screen sizes
- Show how transcripts for audio and video would be displayed
- Show how captions for video would be displayed
- Show how people can play, pause and stop any moving content
- Show how the user can disable animations or aim not to use blinking or flashing content
- Provide a 'skip to content' link.

Part 3

Summary

In this section we have examined the tools and approaches offered by digital design methods for refining a digital product, including how to effectively harness the strengths and weaknesses of the digital medium to build a product that works across a range of devices to deliver the best possible interactive experience for your users. We looked at using information architecture and search engine optimization to bring structure to content and maximize the time users spend on your product, and how we can test the effectiveness of an interface through different product visualizations.

As always in UX design, it is crucial to keep your audience at the forefront, using the iterative nature of digital design processes to develop your understanding of your users and test and refine your product at various stages. Each stage helps you break down the overall brief and focus on the task at hand in order to gradually build up a complete solution.

71 Hi-fi desktop mock-up for joinery design consultants Ecovia, London – an early version that was not used.

72 Hi-fi desktop and mobile mock-ups for Sam's Café, London.

Notes

Bold numbers refer to pages where citations appear.

4: Rob Walker (2003), 'The Guts of a New Machine', *New York Times Magazine*, https://www.nytimes.com/2003/11/30/magazine/the-guts-of-a-new-machine.html.

6: Nielsen Norman Group (2016), *Don Norman on the Term 'UX'* (video, 2 mins.), https://www.nngroup.com/videos/don-norman-term-ux/.

6, 9: Nielsen Norman Group (2019), *The Immutable Rules of UX (Jakob Nielsen Keynote)* (video, 39 mins.), https://www.nngroup.com/videos/rules-ux/.

Part 1: Methods and approaches

12: Hundreds of different approaches. Design Methods Finder, https://designmethodsfinder.com/.

14: IDEO, https://designthinking.ideo.com/.

15: GV, 'The Design Sprint', https://www.gv.com/sprint/.

17: Diana Mounter (2016), 'How to Empower Designers to Code', *Creative Bloq*, https://www.creativebloq.com/web-design/empower-designers-code-41619919.

18, 19: Design Council (2019), 'Framework for Innovation: Design Council's Evolved Double Diamond', https://www.designcouncil.org.uk/our-work/skills-learning/tools-frameworks/framework-for-innovation-design-councils-evolved-double-diamond/.

20: Gillian Crampton Smith's basics of good interaction design. Bill Moggridge (2007), *Designing Interactions*, Cambridge, MA: MIT Press.

For more on interaction design, see Bruce Tognazzini (2014), 'First Principles of Interaction Design (Revised & Expanded)', AskTog: Interaction Design Solutions for the Real World, https://www.asktog.com/atc/principles-of-interaction-design/.

21: The waterfall approach … is 'only appropriate for some types of system'. Ian Sommerville (2016), *Software Engineering*, 10th ed., Global edition, Pearson Education.

22: See also Kent Beck et al. (2001), 'The Agile Manifesto', Agile Alliance, https://www.agilealliance.org/agile101/the-agile-manifesto/.

35: Damian O'Malley and Steven Stark (2008), 'The Brief for the Sistine Chapel', https://workshop.marketing/wp-content/uploads/2018/06/TheBrieffortheSistineChapel.pdf.

36: Lorinda Mamo (n.d.), Alara Design Studio, https://www.alaradesignstudio.com/ (accessed 8 September 2022).

43: Ben Beaumont-Thomas (2015), 'Holly Herndon: The Queen of Tech-Topia', interview, *Guardian*, https://www.theguardian.com/music/2015/apr/26/holly-herndon-platform-interview-queen-of-tech-topia-electronic-music-paradise-politics.

Jeremy Gordon (2014), 'Holly Herndon Breaks Up with the NSA in Video for New Song "Home"', Pitchfork, https://pitchfork.com/news/56712-holly-herndon-breaks-up-with-the-nsa-in-video-for-new-song-home/.

Metahaven, dir. (2014), *Holly Herndon – Home* (music video, 7 mins.), https://www.youtube.com/watch?v=I_3mCDJ_iWc.

44: Marshall McLuhan and Quentin Fiore (2008), *The Medium Is the Massage*, London: Penguin Books.

44: Martin Lister (2009), *New Media: A Critical Introduction*, 2nd ed., London and New York: Routledge.

46: Tinder (2019), Swipe Night, interactive event, https://tinderswipenight-entry.com/.

46: BBDO New York, 'Thinx: MENstruation', https://bbdo.com/work/5daa0425f1e61ddc75b5a8c0.

46, 47: Danah Boyd (2014), *It's Complicated: The Social Lives of Networked Teens*, New Haven and London: Yale University Press.

47: Kranzberg's first rule of technology. Melvin Kranzberg (1986), 'Technology and History: "Kranzberg's Laws"', *Technology and Culture* 27, no. 3, pp. 544–60.

47: William Gibson in 'The Science in Science Fiction' (2018), *Talk of the Nation*, NPR, https://www.npr.org/2018/10/22/1067220/the-science-in-science-fiction?t=1642607883243.

49: Dominic Wilcox, 'No Place Like Home GPS Shoes', https://www.dominicwilcox.com/gpsshoes.htm.

50: Rafael Lozano-Hemmer, '*Remote Pulse*', https://lozano-hemmer.com/remote_pulse.php.

51: United Visual Artists, '*Topologies #1*', https://www.uva.co.uk/features/topologies1.

51: Jacquard by Google, https://atap.google.com/jacquard/.

52: Elas Duas, @elasduas.

53: 'Artist "Vandalises" Snapchat's AR Balloon Dog Sculpture' (2017), BBC News, https://www.bbc.co.uk/news/technology-41524550.

54: 'Olafur Eliasson', Acute Art, https://acuteart.com/artist/olafur-eliasson/.

54: 'Tomás Saraceno', Acute Art, https://acuteart.com/artist/tomas-saraceno/.

55: PAN Studio, 'Hello Lamp Post', http://panstudio.co.uk/project/hello-lamp-post/.

'Hello Lamp Post' (2013), Playable City, https://www.playablecity.com/projects/hello-lamp-post/.

55: BBDO New York, 'Thinx: MENstruation', https://bbdo.com/work/5daa0425f1e61ddc75b5a8c0.

Part 2: Knowing your audience

58: Daniel Miller (2009), *Stuff*, Cambridge, UK: Polity Press, p. 113.

58: Caroline Criado Perez (2019), *Invisible Women: Exposing Data Bias in a World Designed for Men*, London: Chatto & Windus.

60: junh3 (2021), 'The Instagram Ads Facebook Won't Show You', Signal blog, https://signal.org/blog/the-instagram-ads-you-will-never-see/.

64: Russell L. Ackoff (1989), 'From Data to Wisdom', *Journal of Applied Systems Analysis* 16, pp. 3–9.

69: Carly Fiorina (2004), 'Information: The Currency of the Digital Age', opening speech at Oracle OpenWorld, San Francisco, https://www.hp.com/hpinfo/execteam/speeches/fiorina/04openworld.html.

71: 'The History of Symbols: ISOTYPE' (2012), A Short Introduction to Graphic Design History, http://www.designhistory.org/Symbols_pages/isotype.html.

Wim Jansen (2009), 'Neurath, Arntz and ISOTYPE: The Legacy in Art, Design and Statistics', *Journal of Design History* 22, no. 3, pp. 227–42, https://doi.org/10.1093/jdh/epp015.

Otto Neurath (1933), *Empiricism and Sociology*, quoted in Per Mollerup (2015), *Data Design: Visualising Quantities, Locations, Connections*, London: Bloomsbury Visual Arts, p. 13.

72, 73: Richard Saul Wurman, Loring Leifer, David Sume, et al. (2001), *Information Anxiety 2*, expanded and updated ed., Indianapolis: Que.

73: Stephen Kosslyn (2006), *Graph Design for the Eye and Mind*, Oxford and New York: Oxford University Press.

75: Per Mollerup (2015), *Data Design: Visualising Quantities, Locations, Connections*, London: Bloomsbury Visual Arts.

75: Cole Nussbaumer Knaflic (2015), *Storytelling with Data: A Data Visualization Guide for Business Professionals*, Hoboken, NJ: Wiley, pp. 12, 184.

88: User stories in the agile process. Mike Cohn (2004), *User Stories Applied: For Agile Software Development*, Boston: Addison-Wesley.

Part 3: Refining your product

106, 108: Marshall McLuhan and Quentin Fiore (2008), *The Medium Is the Massage*, London: Penguin Books, p. 81.

107: Jonathan Harris and Greg Hochmuth (2015), *Network Effect*, MIT Docubase, https://docubase.mit.edu/project/network-effect/. See also the project website: https://networkeffect.io/.

108: Douglas Rushkoff (2011), *Program or Be Programmed: Ten Commands for a Digital Age*, Berkeley, CA: Soft Skull Press.

Mele Koneya and Alton Barbour (1976), *Louder Than Words: Nonverbal Communication*, Interpersonal Communication series, Columbus, OH: Merrill.

115: Beyond Words Studio, *Plane Talking*, https://beyondwordsstudio.com/our-work/plane-talking/.

116: Alan Cooper (2004), *The Inmates Are Running the Asylum*, 2nd ed., Indianapolis: Sams Publishing, p. 19.

123: Eloise Calandre, https://www.eloisecalandre.com/.

132: Chao Liu, Ryan W. White, and Susan Dumais (2010), 'Understanding Web Browsing Behaviors through Weibull Analysis of Dwell Time', *SIGIR '10: Proceedings of the 33rd International ACM SIGIR Conference on Research and Development in Information Retrieval*, pp. 379–86, https://doi.org/10.1145/1835449.1835513.

See also Jakob Nielson (2011), 'How Long Do Users Stay on Web Pages?', Nielsen Norman Group, https://www.nngroup.com/articles/how-long-do-users-stay-on-web-pages/.

138, 139: 'How to Make a User Flow Diagram' (2022), Creately blog, https://creately.com/blog/diagrams/user-flow-diagram/.

144: Ross Johnson (n.d.), 'Paper Prototyping for Design Sprints', 3.7 Designs blog, https://3.7designs.co/blog/2019/02/15/paper-prototyping-design-sprints/.

148: *Understanding Accessibility Requirements for Public Sector Bodies* (2018), London: Central Digital and Data Office, Cabinet Office, https://www.gov.uk/guidance/accessibility-requirements-for-public-sector-websites-and-apps (last updated 22 August 2022).

'W3C Accessibility Standards Overview' (2022), W3C, https://www.w3.org/WAI/standards-guidelines (last updated 29 June 2022).

'Website Accessibility Under Title II of the ADA' (2007), chapter 5 of *ADA Best Practices Thool Kit for State and Local Governments*, Washington, DC: Americans with Disabilities Act, Civil Rights Division, U.S. Department of Justice, https://www.ada.gov/pcatoolkit/chap5toolkit.htm.

Further reading

User experience design

Allanwood, Gavin, and Peter Beare (2019). *User Experience Design: A Practical Introduction*. 2nd ed. London: Bloomsbury.

Cooper, Alan, Robert Reimann, David Cronin, and Christopher Noessel (2014). *About Face: The Essentials of Interaction Design*. 4th ed. Indianapolis: Wiley.

Hartson, Rex, and Pardha S. Pyla (2019). *The UX Book 2: Agile UX Design for a Quality User Experience*. 2nd ed. Cambridge, MA: Morgan Kaufmann.

Lang, James, and Emma Howell (2017). *Researching UX: User Research*. Victoria, Australia: Sitepoint.

Norman, Donald A. (2004). *Emotional Design: Why We Love (or Hate) Everyday Things*. New York: Basic Books.

Design methods

Brown, Tim, and Barry Katz (2019). *Change by Design*. Rev. ed. New York: HarperCollins.

Case, Steve (2017). *The Third Wave: An Entrepreneur's Vision of the Future*. New York: Simon & Schuster.

Cleese, John (2020). *Creativity: A Short and Cheerful Guide*. London: Hutchinson.

Figueiredo, Lucas Baraças, and André Leme Fleury (2019). 'Design Sprint versus Design Thinking: A Comparative Analysis.' *Capa* 14, no. 5, pp. 23–47. https://revista.feb.unesp.br/index.php/gepros/article/view/2365.

Frascara, Jorge (1997). *User-Centred Graphic Design: Mass Communications and Social Change*. London: Taylor & Francis.

Frascara, Jorge (2004). *Communication Design: Principles, Methods, and Practice*. New York: Allworth.

Gibbons, Sarah (2016). 'Design Thinking 101.' Nielsen Norman Group. https://www.nngroup.com/articles/design-thinking/.

Howkins, John (2020). *Invisible Work: The Hidden Ingredient of True Creativity, Purpose and Power*. London: September Publishing.

Knapp, Jake, John Zeratsky, and Braden Kowitz (2016). *Sprint: How To Solve Big Problems and Test New Ideas in Just Five Days*. New York: Simon & Schuster. https://www.thesprintbook.com.

McDougall, Sean (2012). 'Co-Production, Co-Design, Co-Creation: What Is the Difference?', Stakeholder Design. https://www.stakeholderdesign.com/co-production-versus-co-design-what-is-the-difference/.

Noble, Ian, and Russell Bestley (2018). *Visual Research: An Introduction to Research Methodologies in Graphic Design*. 3rd ed. London: Bloomsbury Visual Arts.

Norman, Donald A. (2013). *The Design of Everyday Things*. Rev. and expanded ed. Cambridge, MA: MIT Press.

Design systems

Google. Material Design. https://material.io/design.

GOV.UK Design System. https://design-system.service.gov.uk/.

Saarinen, Karri (n.d.). 'Building a Visual Language: Behind the Scenes of Our New Design System.' Airbnb Design. https://airbnb.design/building-a-visual-language/.

Salesforce. Lightning Design System. https://www.lightningdesignsystem.com/.

Suarez, Marco, Jina Anne, Katie Sylor-Miller, et al. (2017). *Design Systems Handbook*. DesignBetter.co by InVision. https://www.designbetter.co/design-systems-handbook.

Understanding the client

Belsky, Scott (2010). *Making Ideas Happen*. London and New York: Portfolio Penguin.

Fielding, Daryl (2022). *The Brand Book*. London: Laurence King.

Strat&Art (2014). *Every Project Starts with a Brief. But...* Video, 26 mins. https://www. youtube.com/watch?v=3X6SdMRag-Y.

Multiplatform space

Krotoski, Aleks (2013). *Untangling the Web: What the Internet Is Doing to You*. London: Faber & Faber.

Moggridge, Bill (2010). *Designing Media*. Cambridge, MA: MIT Press.

Powers, William (2010). *Hamlet's Blackberry*. New York: HarperCollins.

Putnam, Robert D. (2007). *Bowling Alone*. New York: Simon & Schuster.

Rushkoff, Douglas (2014). *Present Shock: When Everything Happens Now*. New York: Current.

Shirky, Clay (2009). *Here Comes Everybody*. London: Penguin.

Turkle, Sherry (2017). *Alone Together*. 3rd ed. New York: Basic Books.

Data collection

D'Ignazio, Catherine, and Lauren F. Klein (2020). *Data Feminism*. Cambridge, MA: MIT Press.

Presenting data visually

Battle-Baptiste, Whitney, ed. (2018). *W. E. B. Du Bois's Data Portraits: Visualizing Black America*. New York: Princeton Architectural Press.

McCandless, David (2014). *Knowledge Is Beautiful*. London: William Collins; New York: Harper Design.

Posavec, Stefanie, and Giorgia Lupi (2016). *Dear Data*. London: Particular Books.

Tufte, Edward R. (1990). *Envisioning Information*. Cheshire, CT: Graphics Press.

Storytelling

Huber, Amy M. (2018). *Telling the Design Story: Effective and Engaging Communication*. New York: Routledge.

Loizou, Andreas (2022). *The Story Is Everything: Mastering Creative Communications for Business*. London: Laurence King.

Rehkopf, Max (n.d.). 'User Stories with Examples and a Template.' Atlassian. https://www.atlassian.com/agile/ project-management/user-stories.

Schepers, Nicolas (2017). '8 Lessons on Creating Strong User Journey Narratives.' U-Sentric Blog. https://medium.com/ @usentric/8-lessons-on-creating-strong-user-journey-narratives-57cccf69f759.

Understanding the user and user testing

Bell, Judith, and Stephen Waters (2018). *Doing Your Research Project: A Guide for First-Time Researchers.* 7th ed. London: Open University Press.

Buley, Leah (2013). *The User Experience Team of One: A Research and Design Survival Guide*. Brooklyn, NY: Rosenfeld Media.

Krug, Steve (2014). *Don't Make Me Think, Revisited: A Common Sense Approach to Web Usability*. 3rd ed. San Francisco: New Riders.

Kuniavsky, Mike, Elizabeth Goodman, and Andrea Moed (2012). *Observing the User Experience: A Practitioner's Guide to User Research*. 2nd ed. Waltham, MA: Morgan Kaufmann.

Portigal, Steve (2013). *Interviewing Users: How to Uncover Compelling Insights*. Brooklyn, NY: Rosenfeld Media.

Unger, Russ, and Carolyn Chandler (2012). *A Project Guide to UX Design: For User Experience Designers in the Field or in the Making*. 2nd ed. San Francisco: New Riders.

Designing a digital interface

Moggridge, Bill (2007). *Designing Interactions*. Cambirdge, MA: MIT Press.

Stopher, Ben, John Fass, Eva Verhoeven, and Tobias Revell (2021). *Design and Digital Interfaces: Designing with Aesthetic and Ethical Awareness*. London: Bloomsbury Visual Arts.

Yablonsky, Jon (2020). *Laws of UX: Using Psychology to Design Better Products and Services*. Sebastopol, CA: O'Reilly.

Search engine optimization

Enge, Eric, Stephan M. Spencer, and Jessie Stricchiola (2015). *The Art of SEO: Mastering Search Engine Optimization*. 3rd ed. Sebastopol, CA: O'Reilly.

'What Is SEO / Search Engine Optimization?' (2010). Search Engine Land. https://searchengineland.com/guide/what-is-seo.

Accessibility

'Designing for Web Accessibility' (2015). W3C. https://www.w3.org/WAI/tips/designing (last updated 9 January 2019).

'Understanding WCAG 2.1' (2018). GOV.UK Service Manual. https://www.gov.uk/service-manual/helping-people-to-use-your-service/understanding-wcag (last updated 24 May 2022).

Index

Page numbers in *italics* indicate illustration captions.

Credits

Bold numbers refer to pages where images appear (t: top, b: bottom, l: left, r: right).

Acknowledgements

I would like to thank Kara Hattersley-Smith and Liz Faber for commissioning the book, Jodi Simpson for her patience in editing, Sophie Hartley for helping to source all the amazing images, Allan Sommerville for expressing the principles of the book through his design, and Tristan Stevens for his feedback. Thanks also to Sophie for giving me the space to write this book.